The
Sorcerer
of
Bolinas
Reef

The
Sorcerer
of
Bolinas
Reef

Charles Reich

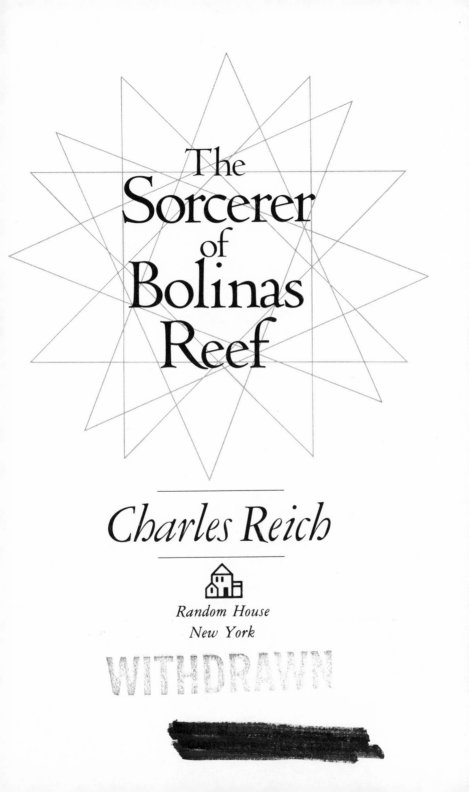

Random House
New York

The simplest person who in his
integrity worships God, becomes God . . .

—RALPH WALDO EMERSON

*For my Father
and Mother*

Spiritual Mentors

☆

Michael Guilkey

Gregory Marriner   *James Roediger*

☆

Roger Ressmeyer

CONTENTS

Thou Reader

Thou reader throbbest life and pride
and love the same as I,
Therefore for thee the following chants.

—WALT WHITMAN

There comes a time when the need for truth is so great, when lies and distortions have made ourselves, and the selves of those we love, and the things we believe in, so unrecognizable, that at any cost we must go in search of the truth, no matter how long and hard and lonely the road. There comes a time when we realize we are like people who continue to live together but have long since lost the ability to look at each other. There comes a time when our need to regain the power to love is so great that at any risk and any price we must regain that power.

The
Futurama

One

In 1939, at the New York World's Fair, I stood in a long line, an eager, excited boy of eleven, to see the General Motors Futurama. The line slowly ascended a sloping outdoor ramp, then a higher ramp, and finally disappeared inside a twenty-first century building. One by one we were seated in soft, comfortable armchairs which moved on an endless belt. A voice that seemed to be that of a cultured, educated man who had seen beyond our time came intimately from a speaker placed near my ear as I leaned back in the moving chair. Swiftly a visionary panorama unfolded: beautiful countryside, neat and well spaced suburbs, and an ultramodernistic city. Superb highways carried traffic smoothly; trucks and faster traffic moved on an inner belt and slower local vehicles on a parallel outside belt. In the heart of the city pedestrians walked on a street level completely separated from the traffic below. It was orderly and serene, a calm and inspiring assurance of human progress. I saw it twice and would go back again today if those traveling armchairs could still take me to that hopeful world.

In New York City, when I was growing up during the thirties, the Futurama was already being built. Those great monuments to the modern vision—the Empire State Building, the Chrysler Building, Radio City Music Hall, the Daily News Building, Sixty Wall Tower and the George Washington and Triboro Bridges—excited hope in me whenever I saw them, silvery on a clear day or gleaming in the night. The Art Deco interiors of the period, such as the lobby of the Music Hall, and sculptures, such as the Atlas on Fifth Avenue, were equally inspiring. And the parkways, curving out from the city in landscaped swards of green, allowed us to drive on the Futurama's highways for picnics at Lake Mohansic or Jones Beach.

Oh, how much we believed in, in those days. My parents were modern people, and the things we loved most were the new inventions: moving stairs in a department store, high-speed elevators, the mechanical wonders at the Automat, the expressway along the west side of Manhattan, the great ocean liners at their docks, the way the symphony orchestra rose up out of nowhere at Radio City Music Hall. We revered Franklin Delano Roosevelt, we believed in public housing, playgrounds, great new hospitals, modern and progressive schools, the TVA, streamlined trains and medical research. When I started high school, the seniors gave their own commencement program, entitled "For Ours Are the Coming Years."

It was at Jones Beach, on a Sunday in December 1941, that we turned on the car radio to catch the Philharmonic Symphony broadcast for the drive home and heard instead the first bulletins of the bombing of Pearl Harbor. And after that first shocking event the future that I could see as a boy was engulfed by a reality that no one wanted—the graceful skyscrapers crowded by flat, ugly monoliths, the parkways choked by traffic, the site of the world's fair itself a twisted nightmare of monstrous interchanges in the forlorn and dusty reaches of the city. One does not have to look to the wars that followed or to the corruption of government or to the decline of faith in America to see the loss of the vision. It is there, all of it, in those New York buildings, bridges and parkways, sad reminders of a dream that has not yet come true.

Fourteen years later, in 1953, I was seated in a high-ceilinged office near the rear corner of the United States Supreme Court building in Washington, D.C. A connecting door led to the imposing but unadorned room where Justice Hugo L. Black was at work. I was one of his law clerks. Here I was, in the great temple of justice at the side of a man who embodied the same optimism and intensity of faith in America that the world's fair had expressed. But the white marble Supreme Court building was now an isolated outpost in a threatening world. Outside the tall window behind my desk the Futurama vision was nowhere to be seen.

From my window I looked out at the despairing slums of Washington, where people dragged themselves through lives that seemed closed to hope. But that was not the only decay I saw. In the Capitol, on the other side of our building, Congress was obsessed with closing down free speech and new ideas while building a repressive security-state. Sometimes I would go over to watch Senator McCarthy and experience firsthand the atmosphere of fear and conformity which had taken over much of our government. The nation had been invaded by armaments for "national defense," by uncontrolled corporate growth, and by real estate developments smothering the countryside. The Court and that fragile old document the Constitution stood as a not always reliable wall against the inhuman trend. Time after time we read briefs and listened to arguments involving people who had been persecuted, exiled or destroyed by their own government.

In those days the Court met in conference on Saturdays, and when Justice Black emerged in the late afternoon, that man of calm and sweet temperament was sometimes flushed with anger as the Court sided with oppression and failed to trust in the Bill of Rights. After a session like that we would drive home together to his beautiful old house in Alexandria. The Justice would never be bitter, but he was profoundly concerned. He feared, feared deeply, for the country he loved so much. He feared that it had lost faith in itself, that it had forgotten its guiding principles.

Over dinner or up in the Justice's study filled with books he loved and marked up and knew almost by heart, we talked about American history and what was now happening to the country. Speaking with his quiet passion Justice Black talked of what he called our ancient liberties, the "thou shalt nots" by which the Bill of Rights intended to restrain the government from acts of tyranny. Justice Black's voice was often a lonely symbol of dissent in the hushed and solemn courtroom.

More than twenty years pass—years as a young lawyer in Washington, D.C., and as a teacher at Yale—and now I am again by a window, but the time is the present, and I look out not at the slums of Washington, but south over the city rooftops of San Francisco. The fog is coming over from the unseen coast to the west, and the reflection of the sunset is visible like tiny sparks of flame in the windows of the buildings across the Bay in Oakland. I am seated at a table in my apartment, in a room filled with plants and pictures and small magical objects that serve as household gods. For a moment I recall the struggle for personal survival and growth during the last few years, and the almost unbelievable changes we have all seen.

The evening news on television tells the story, for while the news remains interesting, indeed fascinating, I no longer imagine that the political leaders or commentators who parade across the screen will have greater knowledge or better answers than anyone else. Those at the top of the governmental or business or educational hierarchies are no longer believed or listened to, and do not seem to grasp the full dimensions of what is taking place. They are out of touch with the people and with reality. The measures they propose seem puny and irrelevant in the face of rising chaos. Life is closing down on much of our hopes, comfort, safety and freedom. Events have an epic, biblical quality. A whole nation is falling into darkness.

People on the streets are showing the fear and the strain. They have been drained of belief, energy, motivation. There is a vast discontent; unrest and mistrust abound. The very core of our lives is insecure. Already a kind of craziness is evident in a wide range of individuals, something akin to the madness brought on by torment, a despairing light-headedness both funny and dangerous—as if in response to too much hurt and too many irrational events. Many people are loosed from their moorings and are searching or drifting.

Something is happening that is larger and deeper, more purposeful and more menacing than anything we have yet recognized or acknowledged to each other. It is coming toward us at an accelerating rate of speed, looming upwards from the depths. Now our senses are alert to the onrushing unknown, but we already fear it may be too late. Whatever it is, we have not begun fully to understand it. It is too large in scale, too penetrating into our interiors, too independent of and indifferent to anything we believe in.

When our land becomes alien to us, when our lives are marked by fear and pain, we have a choice. We can attempt to build a private fortress, keeping the world out with fences, burglar alarms and guard dogs. Or we may attempt to understand what is happening, and seek to confront it together.

Can we see the road we are traveling? Can we see events and news and personal experiences all as part of a pattern that makes sense, that is coming from somewhere and headed for somewhere? Can we locate our most inner lives in a logical story that moves through time and space?

After the Second World War, we began to lose our way, as a country and as a people. In the fifties and sixties, many efforts were made to turn our society around, through political change and institutional reform. Civil rights, the Vietnam war, and concern with poverty and inequality were rallying points. But reform and radical politics did not work. Gradually we were compelled to see that the loss of direction was too deep. It was inside of us. Not just our social system alone, but the human part of that system as well had gone wrong. There would be no real change unless and until people themselves changed. We had to begin with ourselves.

Underneath this realization lay the fact that our inner, most defended core of self had become directly vulnerable to the destructive power of an uncontrolled economic machine. Our society dominates self: controlling, distorting and obliterating our feelings, knowledge and potential. We are programmed and manipulated so that the very essence of what we believe to be ourselves might well cease to be so.

Our alienated selves, multiplied into an entire population, have become ungovernable and ungoverning, so that a majority of our national problems can be seen as enlargements of the hostility, irrationality and isolation that we cannot help but create.

To be subject to alienation is to lose self-knowledge. The more our minds, thought processes, feelings, and capacities become the victims of damage and depletion, the less we are able to remember that we were or could be different. All of our beliefs about ourselves, other people, and the surrounding "reality" of the world change without our knowing it.

Even if we fully accept the idea of how human beings have lost their autonomy, even if it forms a major tenet of our intellectual beliefs, we may still be utterly unable to recognize the forms alienation takes inside of ourselves and others. Our most personal feelings and our very nature may be the disguised agents of an alien power.

Faced with an increasingly hostile world, we have built defenses around ourselves. Retreating but carrying the false self with us into our retreat, we resign ourselves to being unhappy, powerless, alone, and unable to change, rather than rebelling in anger.

In this condition we are within a prison that is like no

other we have ever known. The prison is divided into separate cells for each individual—cells that we carry around with us everywhere, covering up our bodies and faces and minds. So although we appear to move freely—unfettered and unguarded through our daily routines and through our lives—each of us might be locked into a cell that covers us completely.

The walls of the prison are not made of metal or concrete, they consist of barriers to awareness. The walls do not cut off our movements or sight or hearing, they cut off our capacity to know. We are kept prisoners by the fact that we know nothing else but the artificial world in which we are forced to live and take part. There is nowhere to go, no different way of being or feeling, because we are cut off from seeing it.

But there may be a way out. As we begin to see what is happening to us and to our society, we realize that it may be possible for us to change in a way, and to a degree that never has been possible before. We have already within us the ability to change.

It is this discovery that underlay the new consciousness movement of the late sixties. During those years some people who saw the ineffectuality of political change began to seek an alternative answer. They tried the path of personal change, encouraged the growth of a new awareness. The early pioneers of change were outsiders, dropouts, misfits, kids. Like pioneers, they experienced hardship and suffering. What they did discover was that people can change, that there are unexplored places in all of us, and that we can seek change by a journey toward self-knowledge.

In his 1855 preface to the first edition of *Leaves of Grass,* Whitman called upon himself to write a new kind of poetry fit for a new country. In *Democratic Vistas,* Whitman asked others to produce an American literature, a literature that would express the continued unfolding of the American vision. In writing this book, it has been my ambition to be one of those who answers Whitman's call. For I see these savage days of doubt and madness as a supreme moment in the American experience. In the earlier years of this century, those who answered Whitman were the writers of the social novel, the novel of people gripped by social and economic forces, people who were society's victims. In the 1970's the poetry of America, the novel of society, must take a new and more complex and more intensely personal form. But I deliberately seek the strength of the older tradition. And this allows me to address the reader in a special way. Emerson, Whitman, Melville, Hawthorne wrote seriously about the soul, and they sought in their writings to address the soul in the reader. I wish to do likewise, to allow for the possibility that there is a real part of us that perhaps has not been spoken to for a long time.

If alienation isolates each of us in a separate prison cell, it may well be that I can only know my own piece of the puzzle, and can best learn from what I see through the lens of my own life. My quest leads me to consider emotional conditions as highly important data. Good and bad feelings have an objective cause, not necessarily apparent to us, but always worthy of our respectful attention, having an important scientific significance. For I believe that there is a way to discover essential truth by putting back together what society may have wrongfully forced apart, that wholeness may tell us something that we can never learn from the separate parts of our lives.

It is time to begin our journey. As we sit opposite each

other by the window in my San Francisco apartment, we can look out and see the lights of the city coming on and the fog swirling down. We have the whole night ahead of us. The refrigerator is stocked with provisions. Our two armchairs become the traveling chairs of the Futurama. From them we will see the country as it was, and the road we have traveled since. Gently, imperceptibly, the chairs begin to move. I put a candle in the window as the night falls.

My father was a doctor in New York City when he married my mother in the late 1920's. They were both quite idealistic, believing that a life devoted to science and healing would offer them a good chance for happiness. I was born in 1928. My father worked hard at his medical practice; my mother helped him and tried to create a social life for the two of them, gradually developing a career of her own in nursery school administration. My brother Peter was born in 1931.

As a child I lived some of the time in a magical world and dreamed about the future in a magical way. I spent many of my happiest moments daydreaming. I was always interested in government, often dreaming of being President of the United States and thinking of all the things I would do to improve the country. At other times the United States seemed too small, so I imagined myself as Captain Charles, ruler of the universe, with rocket ships and a magic wand. I loved books, especially stories about adventure, exploration, and mystery; I had one set of daydreams in which I led a romantic life like a hero in the stories. Another side of me loved nature, especially the mountains. Still another side of me was devoted to music, and I pictured myself as a great symphonic composer, wildly conducting my own works before an enthralled audience.

Alone on a three-hour walk in the city, I could enjoy these daydreams in marvelous detail, hating to be interrupted when it was time for dinner.

As a boy I pursued each of these dreams and continued to do so through high school. The nature dream was the one that first became a reality. In the summers we would go to our family's house in the Adirondacks. By the time I was eleven, I had climbed the highest peak in New York State, Mount Marcy. For years, along with my brother and one or two friends, I hiked and climbed and explored not only marked trails, but also many trailless wilderness areas where we could give our own names to nameless peaks and imagine that we were the first ever to set foot in that area. The woods made me marvelously happy. Hiking and camping was in no way as popular as it is today. We had the woods and mountains and streams almost to ourselves. We had adventures in rain and cold and clouds, adventures that were among the most satisfying moments of my life. To sleep out on a rocky peak with silence all around and black spaces and stars above was to feel oneself a traveler in the universe.

Along with the dreamer was the rebel. In some furious, primitive way, I resisted the effort to civilize me. I would rather not do it at all than do it "their" way. I hated to be hurried, hated pressure, hated to conform. The warrior in me grew ever stronger.

When I could do something really well, I loved doing it and I loved myself for doing it so well. The schools I went to—first nursery school, then a small progressive elementary school, then a progressive high school; all private and experimental—provided an environment in which I flourished. I enjoyed every minute in school except when athletics took place. School was the hopeful, exciting, satisfying part of my life. Home was a far less happy place, a place of tension, anger, powerlessness for me, violent encroachments and disturbances, restless activity and inactivity.

Out of the atmosphere of the thirties and early forties —influenced by liberal and progressive people I came to know and listen to, enjoying schools that were experimental and fun and exciting (so that days at school were like being part of a group of co-workers engaged in learning a better way to live together) and filled with a passionate, hopeful idealism that I could have a great life—I had a vision for myself. I wanted to help build a new society, a new community, discover a new way of life. I wanted to know everything about the American experience—the Plains, the Middle West, the Pioneers, the Mountains, the Past. I wanted to contribute to knowledge, to make some scientific discovery or create a new philosophy. I wanted to see the marvelous planned cities of the future. I wanted natural beauty, and peace.

It was possible to imagine a world of progress ahead. Schools would be wonderful places for teachers and students alike. There would be deep respect for nature and history. There would be basic social services for all—hospitals, community housing, social security, theaters and parks. A spirit of working together would make us all friends.

I did not see the dark shadow coming. I saw frightful things in the world, but I did not imagine that they would happen to us. Nazi Germany and Fascist Italy showed that people could be turned into mindless automatons, wildly supporting evil leaders at mass rallies and mechanically carrying out the leaders' commands. It was a combination of science fiction and horror stories, an incarnation of a purely evil future: a technological hell, an entire society that was a prison. I was also very aware of corruption, injustice and prejudice in America, but I never for a moment doubted that decency and intelligence and honesty would win. I loved and believed in the triumph of naive goodness in the film *Mr. Smith Goes to Washington.* I never imagined that the country was in peril. There were enough people to spot the danger, enough who loved America, enough who were intelligent and fair, to guarantee the future.

If I had seen the shape it would come in, if I had imagined its power to deceive, to numb, to control—how I would have cried out in warning to everyone who would listen! I would have made a Radio Speech to the Nation, a speech in the style of the thirties, a speech by a fourteen-year-old boy who rushes to a radio station and somehow convinces them that he must be heard.

I am Charles, age fourteen, and I speak to you in the name of science and freedom, and because we are all in the same danger. It is most desperately urgent that you hear me. An alien power will try to take over our minds and our selves and our country. We can see it from here, but we may not be able to see it once it surrounds us and gets inside us. It will turn our cities into jungles and our land into ugliness and fear, and it will make us strangers to one another.

Hear me before we lose the power to speak and to listen! Hear me before all sense of working together, of community and common conscience are gone! Before long this alien power will make us forget the things we cherish most. It will make us believe that these things never existed and cannot exist, it will offer us fraudulent substitutes. It will cut off our knowledge of one another's pain and loneliness. It will make us such strangers to ourselves that we will be deprived of the knowledge of what is good for us. We will be stripped of life.

I speak before we are all prisoners, before we are all slaves, while we still know the true feeling of freedom. I stand up so you can see that you are not alone.

We may wake up to find ourselves living in an alien land. If we ask, we will be told it is our country, that nothing has changed. We will know that something is wrong, because we will feel so horrible, so empty and isolated, so selfish, so bored, so trapped. But we will blame these feelings on ourselves.

My fellow citizens, all this will happen, is happening, and yet we can survive and yet we can triumph. For in that alien land, we can seek to know ourselves. And if we possess the power of self-knowledge, we can still hear each other, still listen.

Young Lawyer

Two

I remember a grey November day in Washington, D.C., in 1956. Our law firm had just won a famous victory. A corrupt official, who had brazenly stolen public funds and had been convicted, was freed on a technicality which I found in the statutes. The other lawyers who had worked on the case were going to have a victory dinner at the client's expense at Chez Maxime, an exclusive French restaurant. I politely declined. I drove home through the miles of bleak apartment houses feeling no appetite and a hollow emptiness inside. At home I feasted on two hotdogs in solitary splendor and misery.

From 1953 to 1960 I was a young lawyer in Washington, D.C. I was close to the marble buildings where national decisions were made. I saw and was part of a world of high officials, lawyers, apartment houses, middle-class fami'' and single men and women—a world which all of lieved to be at the center, and yet typical, of Ame'

It was a world that confidently believed in itself. But for me, in my mid-twenties, something indefinable was always deeply wrong.

I never for one single moment meant to become a young lawyer. I never meant to be a young bachelor in Washington, D.C., with a job at a high-powered firm, an apartment on Connecticut Avenue, suits and ties from Brooks Brothers, dates with young women, and an open-topped car. I still kept hold of very different dreams, and so in secret I was a spy from another world, able to see that world of Washington, D.C.—the people in it, and even myself in the role of a young lawyer—as a spy might see it, from the inside, but with an outsider's eye. I had not planned on this role of spy in alien territory, and once there, I could not be sure of ever getting away, or ever finding a different world beyond. So in a sense I was not a spy because this was my real life. And for all I know, other people were also spies, but I never found out. We could not open up to one another.

What I had planned on, in a logical, methodical way, was getting an education. It was a time, as now, when young people carefully planned their lives for years ahead, and I fully accepted that idea and carried it out in my own characteristic way.

I wanted to see firsthand how our society was run so that I could eventually teach or write about it, or help in running it. I wanted to learn how to be a professional person in the area of public affairs. I also wanted to force myself out into the "real world," after years of school, so that I would be independent of my family. I wanted to cope and be competent. And finally, I wanted to "cure" myself. I was possessed by dark fears, inadequacies, and compulsions which made me feel that outside of my work I was an immature, sick person. I felt it was long past time for me to be a calm, secure person, with relationships of my own.

Looking back, it was entirely right for me to want the education of becoming a young adult. But I was amazingly wrong in the assumptions I made. I took pride in being as realistic as possible, but to a large extent I ended up misdirecting my energy, being concerned with the wrong things, spending years attempting to master the wrong curriculum. My vision was clearest in the area of public life, and most confused in the areas that were personal.

My life was dominated by a firmly established parent inside of me who saw life as a progression from an uncivilized childhood state to one of maturity. But there was still a child in me who would feel frightened, needful of support from others, gleeful, stubborn, and extreme. I ordered myself to grow up. But there was another part of me that would not accept the orders. It was dissatisfied with grown-up happiness, and was ready to sneak away to hidden pleasures.

The true situation was that I wanted every form of secret as well as acceptable happiness, but believed that in order to get there one must follow the path laid down by society. At the time it did not seem strange to me that the path led away from happiness—toward hard, intense, unrewarding work or toward spending my life in situations that did not feel good. I accepted the doctrine that happiness was a reward for doing one's duty. I believed that if I did well at what society wanted me to do, I would receive happiness because society made good on its promises. I thought that A's in school and weekend work at the office would place me in a position to have the things I really wanted in life, a belief held by many of my generation. I worked at earning happiness, but it did not come. My plan was logical, but every year that I followed it, I found that the things I really wanted were yet further away.

For me, the years in Washington, D.C., became years in Limbo, a time before real living began. Many of my own generation accepted the idea of being in Limbo, even for years, as a valid way of getting to a good place, which we felt surely existed. We sat at desks piled high with work, confident enough that we were going to bring home a great heap of happiness one day. What we did not tell one another was the fact that we had not found what we wanted. I truly believed that everyone but me, or almost everyone, had acquired it.

It was easy to place people in categories different than myself, both above me and below me, because I believed that people came in different species. There were clean, expert, competent people who did well at everything and had fun. There were sweaty, bigoted, uneducated people whose lives were an unending banality. There were neurotic, messed-up people like myself. I felt unequal to everyone, had inflexible standards for myself and others, was intolerant of myself and others.

Today I can see a larger and more organic shape to my overly logical and planned career. But then I did not think I knew how to become a man in the world of Washington. I was looking for a father, looking for people as teachers and models, trying out the role of manhood, holding myself to the highest standards I knew about. It was of the essence of the spirit of the 1950's that the country was thought to be run by those at the center of things, and I wanted to take my place as close to the center as possible. That was a true fifties concept.

In attempting to make a bargain with society, so that if I carried out my plan I would get what I wanted, I was very much the Young Lawyer. I fully expected that society would live up to its half of the bargain. I wanted an exact return on my investment, and I wanted a bonus for working extra hard. If I felt cheated, I would be so intensely concerned with the injury to my legal right that I might ignore a better way of getting what I wanted. I screamed for justice.

Meanwhile, society was not dealing with me fairly, I thought. It had not undertaken to fulfill its promise; the initiative was all on my side. I volunteered myself, hoping to be rewarded.

When I came to Washington it was under the most favorable circumstances imaginable. My personal dreams, my search for wisdom, and my plans for myself all came together in one perfect way: in 1953 I received an appointment as law clerk to Justice Hugo L. Black.

Along with David Vann, the other law clerk, I lived on the ground floor of the Justice's eighteenth-century house in Alexandria. We had breakfast with him in the kitchen, lunch with him in the public cafeteria at the Court, and dinner back home in the elegant old dining room. From early morning until bedtime we talked about the Constitution and the Bill of Rights. I found in Justice Black a person who had a total faith in the fundamental principles of justice. He carried the Constitution in his pocket as if it were the Bible. He was a warm and unpretentious man, and in a very profound way he made us two law clerks his sons for the year. He showed us how to wash dishes "right," but always did most of the dishes himself. He cooked steaks country-style on Sunday. He told us not to drink or smoke while pouring himself a drink—because liquor couldn't hurt a man at his age. He hinted that David could learn some new working habits from me and that I could learn a little about having fun from David. He was always trying tactfully to improve my driving. He made us look up words in the dictionary that we thought we knew the meaning of.

Hugo Black was an authentically great man. In a city that lived by display, power, gossip, and publicity, his way of life was simple and old-fashioned and wholly without artificial trappings. Each deputy assistant secretary of defense might have a chauffeur and a limousine; Justice Black drove his own old green Plymouth. He loved peace and quiet and a few choice friends. He did his own studying and thinking, and wrote his own opinions, sending to the Court library or the Library of Congress for books as he required them. If a phrase in the Constitution needed to be understood in the context of history or philosophy, he read or reread that history and philosophy. He thought every issue through from the beginning. In a world that was "realistic" about power, Justice Black was passionate about justice for each individual, no matter how inconsequential the person might seem to the world. He was utterly uncorrupted and incorruptible. He was powerful because he possessed the power of love—love of the Constitution, of justice, of democracy, of the people, of his family and friends, of his country. While other judges and lawyers often thought primarily about abstract rules and regulations, the first thing Justice Black saw in a case was the human being involved —the human factors, a particular man or woman's hopes and suffering; this became the focus of all his compassion and indignation.

How I gloried in that marvelous year. I knew that it was one of the greatest experiences that any person could ever have. I never stopped marveling that here I was, sitting at dinner with Justice Black and talking about freedom of speech while the Justice divided a steak three ways, and we passed the corn sticks and greens. I told myself: When you recognize a moment that is an authentic part of your dream, you have to give it all the passionate belief that it deserves.

We sat in the kitchen at breakfast, eating the eggs the Justice had cooked, while he read aloud from *The Washington Post* or talked about the Constitution. The sun streamed in through the windows of the small, low-ceilinged, old-fashioned room, that looked out on a garden. There sat the grand old man, in pajamas and bathrobe, his face serious and majestic, talking about the framers of the Constitution and the deep and terrible experience out of which had been born the protections of the Bill of Rights. He foresaw that we would become "a nation of clerks" if we could not remember what it meant to be a free people. And I knew this was my unique and magical moment to sit with the Prophet, the old man of the American Testament, and absorb his stern passion, his belief in truth, and carry it forward when I could.

After my clerkship ended, I wanted to stay in Washington. I went to work for a law office noted for its identification with Yale Law School, New Deal liberalism, and civil liberties.

The firm was an elegant place. I got a spirited greeting from the receptionist when I arrived; then I sat back in my swivel chair, feeling that I was able to cope with the world. It was in many ways a highly privileged existence. Lawyers arrived at work well after the early-morning rush. I would get myself some coffee from the large percolator down the hall and then enjoy the luxury of settling back with *The New*

York Times and the *Post*—even reading the comics.

Sometimes, tilting in my chair, I doodled floor plans for a splendid office suite with a conference room and waiting room on one side, a private library and sitting room on the other—a magnificent corner sanctum for myself, the great man who must under no circumstances be disturbed.

The firm wanted its young men to assume a certain way of life. One was permitted and expected to take care of the necessary amenities of life on office time. I went for haircuts to the barber shop at the Mayflower Hotel. There was seldom a wait. The atmosphere was deferential and luxurious; one's shoes were shined during the haircut, and at the end a black attendant brushed one off from head to foot, helped one on with one's coat, and gratefully accepted a tip. It was easy to enjoy, and I did enjoy it. In a status-conscious city it felt good to feel so privileged.

There was a great sense of importance. Consider a conference with a high government official, along with two senior partners. I strode purposefully from the office, turning around at the door to say impressively, "We'll be at the Department of Justice." We hailed a taxi and got in. Then there was the monumental façade of the building on Constitution Avenue. The marble hallways, the elaborate reception room, the office of the official, an American flag behind his desk, a view of the Capitol Building from the long windows, portraits of predecessors in office and the official himself asking us to be seated. While the other men did most of the talking, and I returned their glances solemnly, I was inwardly telling myself, "This is what everyone wants! This is really living!" Where these men ate lunch, where they went for recreation, what they talked about, and what they wore was what everyone else wanted and tried to copy.

But even in these moments I could not keep up the pretense that everything from arriving in the morning to the haircut to such a conference was really a meaningful experience. What was happening at the conference was so detached from our real feelings as to make it an inhuman thing—no better, really, than listening to announcements by the stewardess on a coast-to-coast airplane trip. The participants spoke lines, they did not communicate. I wish I had dared look someone in the eye or smile at the high official or just yawn.

I liked to work; it was not self-punishment. I simply enjoyed functioning in a way that felt powerful and competent. And I liked the people I worked with in the firm. They were politically liberal, intelligent, sophisticated, lively, entertaining, and excellent lawyers. They were dedicated craftsmen, devoted to their profession. Yet I felt that they, and I, were all victims of our work.

Our work was detrimental to us, in the most profound way. The moments of enjoying work did not last very long. Something about the firm crept in to interfere. The most obvious forms of interference were interruptions, phone calls, distractions. But these had to be expected in a lawyer's life: a lawyer took whatever came along, without priority, form, turn, or order; he had to glory in his ability to play many parts instead of one. No, the trouble went beyond interruptions and multiple tasks.

The atmosphere in the firm was so often full of tension, overconcern, and uncomfortable pressure that it was hard to maintain a high style. More serious still, what I wrote usually met with some objections from the senior men and eventually ended up as a product different from what I had originally written. They always wanted everything put more strongly. I thought I could be powerful and convincing with a serene air, and I hated to see that sort of work turned into overemphasis. I liked to be the law journal scholar simply presenting my point of view.

The opposition were always "those sons of bitches" or "those bastards" or worse. I never felt the need to make the other side seem so evil. But such an objective memorandum would not do. "It isn't positive enough," they would object. "You can put our position more strongly." My own exact voice, then, was not what they wanted to hear. My expression, my thought, must fit larger objectives. I must present an argument with a conviction I did not necessarily feel, an eagerness that was not necessarily in me, a certainty that I might not possess.

Much of my work consisted of talking to people— colleagues, people from outside, public officials. It was much easier than writing, but was not completely satisfying either. All of these people had a professional, or public, self. They all represented a particular interest or point of view, and they took this position with what seemed to be their heart and soul. If positions had been taken in a purely detached manner, there might have been some zone for genuine human contact between the participants. But detachment did not win ball games; everyone must ring with seemingly true belief. After such a performance, there was little room left for a "real" person to show himself. One put one's entire self—writing, voice, manner, personality, personal appeal, even physical stance—at the service of the matter at hand. One coated over one's real self with a public self—every pore covered, if one were really professional, until the public self became first the only visible self, then the only real self.

Whatever they really felt, the other lawyers liked to adopt the appearance of being cynical about the law and its processes, the causes and clients for which they worked, and the firm itself. Deprecation of everything was almost a way of life with them. Winning and losing cases was a game. Questions of justice, wisdom or good policy were irrelevant for lawyers. They were, in one partner's memorable phrase, hired knife-throwers.

But they did not play it as if it were a game. At the heart of their conversations were tension, anxiety, and a total absorption in their work. I could not accept that lack of distance from work, that lack of a sense of irony or humor. They embraced it, they ate and drank it, they knew no moment away from it, it was life and love to them. It was a case of too much.

When I went to lunch with a couple of young lawyers from the firm, there was lots of animated talk, but I was deeply withdrawn. We talked about politics, but it seemed as if they were simply making an effort to sound clever and amusing. The young men waited eagerly for a chance to seize the center of the conversational stage. They did not really listen to each other, they prepared their own remarks for the moment when the person who was speaking finished. They listened only for the purpose of replying. What they said seemed always to be addressed not to the others at the table, but to some invisible judge or authority figure. So even at a casual moment, when there was no authority present, the conversation continued to be an oratory contest, the brilliant speakers impatiently waiting their chance to earn an A in Lunch.

But there was a worse kind of conversation at lunch. This was when some of the senior lawyers were present and the conversation concerned office cases. I disliked this sort of conversation on principle. I felt it breached an unspoken trust: to be a friend to the person with whom you have a meal. It spoiled the relaxaion of lunch or dinner, the chance of enjoying each other. Each man tried to get as much help as possible for his own work. "Let me pick your brains," they would say. It was upsetting to accept a friendly invitation to lunch only to have your companion suddenly turn into an intense interlocutor. I would become inwardly rigid at the violation, and the next day I would buy sandwiches in a delicatessen and have lunch by myself on a park bench.

The lawyer's life had a fundamental lack of limits. This was even made into a virtue. You could be unexpectedly asked to work nights, Saturdays, Sundays. You might arrive in the office and be told to get on a plane and fly to New York. You might be fully occupied with one job and then abruptly put on another with both to be done in the time allotted for one. Work at the firm simply did not include a factor that showed respect for the needs of the individuals. That would have been considered an inexcusable form of softness.

I think that even worse than the violation of spirit was the destruction of consciousness. Few people respected my right to have my own thoughts and feelings for very long. Usually the whole day was one series of things that jangled the mind until it could no longer function. When I spent a long day at the office without access to my thoughts and feelings, I felt that every moment was one of outside pressure. And my real self was driven far inside. This destruction of thought and feeling plus the repressed anger that went with it made it impossible for me to regain any sense of self when the working day was over. You cannot strike your head all day with a hammer and then expect that the person within will want to come out when you get home.

All of this was epitomized when I was summoned to see one of the senior partners, Mr. Henderson. I entered his office and, in response to his gesture, sat down in a chair near the desk; he was writing something and did not look up for several minutes.

The office, beautifully decorated, was dominated by a huge and ornate desk. The desk was, more than anything else, a barrier. No one could sit *with* Mr. Henderson, only before him. From his fortress he could only watch human intercourse, not join in it.

Mr. Henderson asked about a point in a memorandum I had written. There was a sense of urgency about time, which forbade any personal comments. The urgency also meant that from his question to my answer there was supposed to be no pause or moment of thought, as if my response was to be produced electronically. My answer was received without acknowledgment; Mr. Henderson, however, allowed himself a long silence before his next question. The dialogue was edged with a feeling of competition, of scoring points. There was an acute tension I could feel viscerally.

The phone rang and I sat while he talked leisurely and graciously to some personage. This happened all the time. I felt tension within me—I could neither relax, think, nor leave.

The discussion of the memorandum resumed. His comments stressed words like "strategy," "our objective," "tactical." The other side was "the enemy." The judgments we were making took on an air of infinite precision and exactitude, as if every nuance and move could be calculated. The matter at hand grew in importance until it seemed like the world's most vital business, a matter for secrecy, discretion, gravity, and infinite concern.

The phone rang again, and this time the conversation lasted even longer. Feeling so hostile and so powerless, I sought to become an objective observer of the man at the desk. Mr. Henderson was a great liberal, a public-spirited lawyer, a man who had been a dedicated government official and now still helped in many progressive causes. He had started poor and was a self-made man, but he followed a newer pattern: not the business success story but success in college and law school; a climb up the meritocracy; a man of brains, ability, dedication. He was a pragmatist, but also a man of taste and sophistication. He could not be written off as an organization man, a dull man, or a conformist. Why, then, the harsh cynicism, the toughness, the oppressive self-control, the approach to everything by strategy, the need for power over people? The telephone conversation ceased, and his secretary came in to say that someone was waiting to see him. "Keep going on this," he told me, and the interview was ended.

Of all the lawyers at the firm, it was in Mr. Henderson that I sometimes imagined something, far below the surface, that was in some way like me. I am not talking about the Henderson that Washington knew or the other lawyers in the firm knew. I am talking about the person who could not really want the unutterable isolation of having all other people at a distance. Very simply, I imagined that we were people who could have been friends.

There was one part of me who walked through each day at the office with a tense, set determination, numb to the cries of pain or anger within myself. I could bear anything, endure anything, and do my job. The knowledge of this made me proud. I had volunteered to be in this play, and here I was. I could leave at any time. I told myself, accept whatever the job brings with it, so long as you work here. Then there was another part of me which actually felt pain, fear and anger, who could only take so much and then would go into a fury. There was so much pressure. Any of the partners could assign me work, and none checked with the others to see how much my work load totaled. It was up to me to tell a partner no if I was already too busy, but I never knew how much was expected of me, how much anyone else did, or whether my no would be believed or considered a form of malingering. There was so much boredom and waste of time, such as at long conferences where nothing of real substance happened. There was so much to cause anger, delays, explosive frustration, tension, anxiety, rebellion at what seemed to be stupid instructions, a work rhythm of undue hurry and undue delay, an ethic that required one to endure fools, bullies and petty tyrants with silence or even a pleasant smile. Under my tense and straining façade I boiled and seethed. But it was their firm, not mine.

When the invasion of my inner being became too great, I would disappear to one of my sanctuaries. At times I might go to the office library or any of three government libraries, one shabby-quiet in the typical government way, the second fluorescent and modern, the third the library of the Supreme Court. Also, lunch in out-of-the-way places—in a cafeteria within a large government building, in the fussy but delicious Methodist Building cafeteria near the Senate offices, in a restaurant, sometimes with an old friend from another line of work.

In the library of the Supreme Court—ornate, rich, magnificent, and hushed—I could have an immensely long and splendid wooden table to myself and the grave courtesy of attendants; even the washroom was of marble and scrupulously clean. Very few people used the library, and it was open only to former law clerks and members of the Supreme Court bar. It was like the interior of a place of worship, imposing a silence on everybody. Here I could feel like the privileged law clerk again, the private assistant to the Senior Justice, and not like some sweaty and harassed lawyer. Here I could work the way I liked to work, with moments of contemplation, short interruptions to glance idly at the shelved books or recent periodicals; here all was dignity, repose and silence, with ornamented chairs and table lamps, carpeted floor and carved woodwork.

Sometimes the ornate and solemn library invited a soliloquy. One day I opened *The New York Times* before starting work and saw that a woman I had been dating in New York had gotten married. I was sitting at this table, letting life pass me by, I thought to myself. A flood of emotions inundated my mind. With a great effort, I groped for the reassurance of my logical self. Wasn't this work what I should be doing? I asked myself. I did want public service, I did want to learn a craft, I did want to work on something important.

I was actually working on arguments to be presented to a government regulatory agency in a long-drawn-out proceeding involving a license to construct a dam on a navigable river. The problem was profoundly important: issues of conservation, recreation, natural beauty, preservation of salmon runs, electric rates to consumers, and private versus public power were in dispute. To work on this problem was, surely, to be involved in society in a meaningful way. It was the word "meaningful" that was the joke. The more one knew about how decisions were actually made, the more one felt one was laboring only with appearances.

Basically, the decision would be formed by the main forces that existed in the American polity. First, a set of values that put technology, economic progress, and private power high. Second, the organization and bureaucratic processes within the government agency. Third, political influences in the state and in Congress. Fourth, whatever private economic strength could be mustered. All of these were brought to the limited frame of reference and limited independence of a group of commissioners. This was by no means a corrupt process, in the ordinary sense of the word, but it was a process not amenable to mere reason. Reason, arguments, theories could only be of lesser importance in such a process, the sort of thing that would help to rationalize what was otherwise decided. The person who contributed intellect to such a process was helping to create and perpetuate a lie about how things really happened; he was an unintentional conspirator in the cover-up of social truth.

To see how little words meant, written or spoken, one need only visit a Washington hearing of some sort; a good starting place would be Capitol Hill. At a congressional committee hearing a torrent of words pour out, all for effect; Congressmen look and sound like automatons reading statements somebody else wrote; mountains of words pile up, few of them intended to have much meaning. To live among such people—senators, lawyers, officials—was to live in a world where the spoken word meant little and the written word still less (because it wasn't read); to survive meant either to pretend (which many succeeded in doing) or to live in the limbo of cynicism.

Many of my friends fell back on craftsmanship as a justification for their work, virtuosity for its own sake, a job that other professionals could appreciate. Medicine, painting, and physics were also crafts. But the craft must be morally and socially responsible—at least that is what I believed.

And a craft should be fulfilling as a form of self-expression. How could our craft be this when it was carried out, not only without concern for its social consequences, but also under tremendous pressure, urgency, drive—all of which produced not a work of art to be contemplated, but a product fed into the whirring wheels.

I couldn't help but feel the immense wastefulness of pouring so much energy, so many people's time, so much telephoning, typing, printing, traveling, into an activity that was fundamentally without direction. At the firm we spent by far the better part of our lives doing this work; how could that be justified? Was the society as a whole equally engaged in activities with little social value?

The truth was that I was spending my life in ways that were never what I really wanted to do. I did not want to be in Washington, I did not want to work for a law firm or even be a lawyer, I did not feel drawn toward the people I spent time with. I wanted to be somewhere else, doing something totally different, with people who were exciting and adventurous. No matter how hard I tried to believe that my work was a sign of my "maturity," I found myself full of yearning for something else.

Could one make a life out of this? Could one be a hired knife-thrower and enjoy it? For what pay or for what prestige could it make sense for a person to spend his days this way? There was no possibility of personal growth if there was no chance to experiment with life, to have new experiences, to grow in moral strength. In my law practice there was no grandeur, no public service, no commitment to a cause. No people to be close to. No sky, no sea, no forests, no mountains.

My soliloquy in the Supreme Court Library ended. My own little attempt to find pleasure in my work would begin to fail and I would gather up my papers, leave the splendor of the library, and take my work back to the busy and hectic office.

When I went to a government office building by myself, on some errand for the firm, I began to feel that the firm wasn't so bad after all. No matter what the outside of a government building looked like—Greek columns, quonset hut temporary, or contemporary official monumental—the inside would always be the same. I noticed the inevitable Civil Service Regulations posted in fine print on the dead walls, next to the equally inevitable full-color picture of President Eisenhower and room numbers like D-2407, indicating wing number and floor. The lasting impression was of endless hallways and doors, and signs projecting out with room numbers. It was true of all government buildings that if you forgot a room number you would have to return to the front entrance and start again; there was no other point of connection.

Whatever office you went to on business, the atmosphere was the same—the same furnishings, varied a little according to rank—shirt-sleeves—people just putting in time.

Even more pervasive than the interior sameness was the sense of what it meant to be a government employee, for it meant much the same thing whether one was high or low, male or female, in the State Department or the ICC. The higher echelons might have assigned parking places and larger offices, but the materials of their offices were of the same stuff: official-shabby. It was to the agency world, not the world without, that everyone looked. Promotions, efficiency ratings of employees, rules, security checks on employees, small and large intrigues and empire-building— all took place within the agency and constituted the prime stuff of life.

Witness a government cafeteria at lunch. I often ate in one if I was down in a government building at noon. Everyone ate there, from custodial employees to the most senior men, except a few top men who might occasionally go out to a restaurant (but even department heads and commissioners ate in the cafeteria much of the time). Usually the cafeteria was in the basement—a very large, oppressive underground room. The food items seemed to be the same whatever agency one was in. The menu was apparently the same from week to week. The people in the lines seemed all to be watching budgets and waistlines as they pushed trays toward the desserts and then to the cashier. Government men in groups seemed epitomized by white short-sleeved shirts, rounded shoulders, glasses, a peering, amiable look, a whitish appearance of never being outside. They were of no special age—just making the transition from youth to clerkly married thirties to grey-haired career government employees, from downtown apartment houses to small houses in Tacoma Park or Hyattsville or Arlington, to more substantial houses with space for carpentry in the basement and for gardening in the backyard.

The conversation, when one could overhear it, was

partly about the affairs of the agency but also suggested some of the local news sections of *The Washington Post:* new regulations, man loses auto permit, plans for northeast freeway, G-girl robbed, area man gets award, Terps top North Carolina, sale of home building tools at Hechts' in Falls Church Shopping Center, special on tires at Sears.

I often felt that when people looked to the government for answers or programs or leadership or values or social vision—when they expected that the nation could actually be led by something called "the government" in Washington, D.C.—they simply did not imagine the government as I saw it. Perhaps they thought of vigorous and decisive leaders, weighing all the factors and making wise decisions for the good of the nation. What I saw was something very different.

There was nobody to see things clearly or from an objective point of view. Everyone, high or low, was confined to some special and narrow corridor, waiting for coffee breaks and for the noon line at the cafeteria.

Who ran the country then? I learned that there was an elite group, a class that shared certain assumptions and values, and made basic decisions without offering them to anyone as a choice. It was sometimes called the Club. Its members held controlling positions in government, in firms like mine, in the courts, and in the law schools. They were mostly male lawyers from Ivy League schools—all top-notch achievers. Although they were fiercely competitive, and gave the appearance of representing many different sides of the issues of the day, it gradually dawned on me that the values they shared, rather than those they debated, represented the true decisions which governed the country. For example, it was assumed without debate that it was good to be tough. "Tough-minded" was one of the highest words of praise among the members of this elite group. "Hard-nosed" was another favorite. Suppose there was a choice of two courses of action—one in which a foreign country was assumed to be motivated by a sense of the common good, and the other treating the same country far more guardedly, as if its actions were exclusively dominated by a harsh and narrow self-interest. The course of action that won the respect of the Club and received the accolade of being "tough" was the one that assumed everyone was wholly motivated by self-interest. To have higher expectations of people or countries was thought soft-headed, flabby, weak. And so there was an undebated agreement on being as "tough" as possible. The voters were never asked to pass judgment on this assumption, nor were philosophers asked if it was the wisest course of action for dealing with other human beings. The Club was so sure of its values that it considered them axiomatic. Although righteously upholding free speech, they would not seriously listen to anyone who questioned the wisdom of "toughness." Thus the government, the firm, and our major institutions were ruled by an elite group of managers who agreed that it was best and most realistic to always assume the worst about people and nations. This single principle made an immense difference in our foreign policy, our criminal law, our evaluation of people for important jobs, even our methods of training the professionals and managers who were still in school. There was no difference among Republicans and Democrats or between "private" businessmen in corporations and "public" bureaucrats in the government on this vital issue.

I deeply felt that "toughness" was based on a mistaken

view of human beings, that it was in the long run an unwise and unworkable way to live and govern. It could only lead to a destruction of human solidarity, fragmentation into warring factions. In the end perhaps human society could not survive if "toughness" ruled. But I was fearful of speaking out. I felt that if I argued strongly for a belief in the goodness of people, I would be punished by a loss of respect, perhaps a demotion from the higher ranks of the Club, which as a top achiever I was privileged to occupy. I felt I needed to hold on to that status for security because of the special perquisites it brought me, because it was my chief claim to manhood at a time when my personal life did not show the same kind of success.

I sought not to violate my principles in any of my actions or statements, but I felt I must hide this fact under the disguise of "Charlie." My true self was masked by Charlie's smiling, seeming agreeableness that tactfully avoided stirring up useless trouble. If a client at lunch remarked that the hatcheck girl had a "nice ass" I saw nothing to be accomplished by showing my distaste for his coarse treatment of women, and when clients or other lawyers joked about blacks I inwardly raged but kept silent.

During my years at the firm I continued to be close to Justice Black, sometimes going to see him during the day when I should have been working at the firm. The firm never questioned this, and I thought they approved because they assumed I was keeping up a contact with a powerful and important man in a way that would enhance the firm's "insider" reputation. In truth, I was motivated by a desire to be in a more loving, stimulating, and idealistic environment than the firm provided (whenever I could get away with it) and to give friendship to the man I felt was doing the work of fighting for more freedom. In truth, I was "soft." But I believed everyone at the firm liked "Charlie" far better than they would have liked Charles, and so I felt no permission to be Charles, even though I found "Charlie" a stifling and confining role.

The suits I wore expressed my ambivalence. On the one hand, I felt they had to be exactly right. They must be cut in the Ivy League style, come from Brooks Brothers in New York, and be perfectly cleaned and pressed. My necktie had to be conservative, narrow, perfectly knotted. My shirts must be in the button-down style. My shoes had to be polished. Through college I had been indifferent to the style of the clothes I wore, but after law school I learned to feel that this was the "right" way to look. It was the uniform of a Class A Person. Anything else was a class down—more vulgar, more showy, less tasteful, more common. A Class A person was regarded as a member of an elite of well-educated, Ivy League, highly intelligent men. But without the uniform, people would not recognize or respect my status. In a more common-looking suit, the people I met would not know I was a member of the ruling elite, and I would not receive the respect or admiration or recognition to which I felt entitled. I was an officer, not an enlisted man.

But at the same time, suits were like a straitjacket to me. I was always too hot. I always felt scratchy. My shirt collar choked me. My shirts quickly got soiled with perspiration and had to be changed. I always had to be careful not to get my suit wrinkled or spotted or dirty, and not to flatten out the crease in my pants. It was nearly impossible to work or write, and a suit interfered with the free movement of my mind. Nor could my body move naturally. I felt flabby and unhealthy. I yearned for worn blue jeans and an informal shirt, which could make me feel sensual, active, natural —the clothes of a hiker in the woods. But I would have felt acute, self-conscious embarrassment if I had found myself at the office without my suit. Informal clothes would have raised serious doubts about my maturity and good judgment, as if I had strolled into a conference wearing only my underwear.

Just as I chafed under the exhausting restraints of being Charlie, I felt further removed from my true self by the environment of the lawyer world. A taxi to the airport . . . a wait for the plane, sometimes in the commodore's lounge, reserved for important travelers. The plane trip itself . . . another taxi . . . a downtown hotel room strewn with yellow pads and legal papers . . . drinks and dinner in the hotel dining room . . . everything signed for . . . work until midnight, followed by drinks in the room and a fitful sleep . . . breakfast in the hotel dining room . . . a taxi to an office building . . . a long conference with other men who took all of this seriously . . . a taxi to an expensive restaurant four blocks away . . . drinks and then a heavy lunch . . . conversation about golf and football . . . a taxi four blocks back to resume the meeting . . . finally a taxi back to the hotel. All of my senses would be covered over with hotel drinks and hotel food and whatever hotels use instead of fresh air. Sometimes this life could continue for a week, two weeks or even a month. I desperately wished I could take a walk or sit on a bench or wear a T-shirt and blue jeans. Even more, I wanted to stop feeling grown up and responsible. From the moment I left on the trip until I returned, every penny I spent, even for the newspaper, was charged to the client's account. Every quarter I handed a shoeshine man or dollar I put down for a drink was not my own money. And if anyone thinks this was great, I would like to point out one fact. Every motion I made, every word I uttered, every thought I had was also not my own. It belonged to somebody else.

Sometimes two or three lawyers from my office, often accompanied by an important client, would go out together in Washington for an elegant business lunch. The very assembling of the group in the office lobby was quite a process. Usually one of the group was delayed in his office by an extended phone call, so that the group spent a not-altogether-easy five or ten minutes in the lobby in light, strained conversation.

The entry into the restaurant was very ceremonious. The black doorman, elaborately uniformed, received a hearty greeting. So did the headwaiter and the coat-check woman, but the tone was different for each. The greeting given the doorman was the heartiest and most patronizing; for the headwaiter heartiness was more moderate, implying the latter's higher status, and for the coat-check woman there was an obligatory bit of sexual innuendo. The parade into the dining hall (a spacious and sumptuous room) was interrupted by greetings in a booming voice to one or two men seated at other tables, often by titles and always with a great appearance of close friendships: "Morning, Judge," "Good to see you, Commissioner," "Well, Senator! [with plantation-style courtesy] How are you, sir?"

Did the other diners and the waiters and our waiter in particular realize how important we were, as our procession, led by the captain, moved slowly toward a table billowed in fresh linen? That expense was of no concern to us, that the tip might be munificent? That we were well known here by the staff? That the service would be—must be—

hovering, solicitous, discreet? Tourists did not come to this restaurant. The faces at the other tables were those of up-per-level Washington. Some of the faces were handsome, but none were beautiful. They were bland, affable, some-times hard or powerful, but above all practical. The com-mon denominator was that they were all men on business —there was no one reading a book or just enjoying the food or merely watching the scene. Mixed groups were scarce, but there were several tables of ladies—obviously the wives of important men, downtown for shopping or for a meeting of an organization.

The conversation during the three rounds of drinks and the meal followed a definite ritual. First there were stories that ended with a loud laugh: set pieces of first-drink humor. I never told any jokes, but all the older men did, even those whose personalities seemed uncomfortable with humorous stories. Attention and laughter were mandatory. The second round of drinks brought forth longer stories about current personalities and events in Washington; the most important part of these stories was the names men-tioned. The mode of discourse was always stories (even if the speaker was merely repeating something from the morning newspaper, or something a columnist had writ-ten), and the response was a brief comment and then a story in return. The third round of drinks brought out a slightly different type of anecdote, in which the prowess or skill of the speaker or his organization was illustrated. The speaker was the hero of these tales. One reason I never spoke dur-ing this entire part of the lunch was that the conversation seemed to be an effort, first by one and then by another speaker, to get and hold the floor. The speakers waited in line to demand the attention of the group, and I felt it would be rather forward of me also to seek their attention, and wasn't sure if I wanted it anyway.

Ordering food followed the arrival of the third round of drinks. Suddenly the presence of the waiter was commanded. Where had he been all this time? Usually the ordering was matter-of-fact and businesslike, although an occasional out-of-town guest seemed uneasy with the elaborate menu (they were never uneasy with the drinks). The dishes were excellent: soft-shell crabs, imported English sole, crab meat au gratin, sliced filet of beef with a sauce. I would have liked to add an extra vegetable from the other side of the menu—asparagus hollandaise—but I held back. The extra price, while absurdly high by normal standards of dining, would hardly have been noticed in the huge bill. But I quailed at drawing attention to the fact that I was specially interested in the food itself—I shrank from the moment when, the spotlight of attention suddenly on me, I spoke up to the man who was ordering with a special plea for asparagus. (Worse yet was the awful possibility that the arrival of the entire meal would be delayed, and when an explanation was demanded, the waiter would say apologetically, "The gentleman's asparagus. . . .") One of the other men ordered a very good kind of filet of sole, and I found it more expedient and businesslike to say "Make it two."

The food arrived in a great hubbub of three waiters and the captain, an excess of serving dishes, and a vast mound of sweet butter on a large board. The completion of serving marked an important watershed in the conversation. As soon as the elaborate food had been spread and everyone had received what he wanted (including the man with bad digestion who had simply ordered consommé and scrambled eggs, not on the menu and obtained only at fantastic prices) and the absence of a fork had been rectified (this provided the occasion for an imperious summoning of the waiter, demonstrating power, in contrast to the joviality of greeting at the beginning of the meal), the conversation, as if at a signal, was turned to the business at hand. This was the part of the conversation in which I might be expected to participate. But the discussion did not shed new light on anything; how could it, in such a setting, and after three drinks? Instead, the business discussion consisted mostly of emphatic repetitions of mutual declarations about the virtue of the cause and the villainy of the opposition, as well as unsubtle playing up to the important guest (one would think the average client would be put off by this, but the average client loved it). I sat there, waiting to be called upon as an expert, to explain or amplify what the others had said.

What I really wanted, at this particular moment, was to savor the lobster bisque and the filet of sole. I would have liked to discuss the special virtues of the sauce on the filet of sole. But once the food had arrived, everyone showed a total unconcern about it. They sawed away at the filet of sole or other dishes as if they were meat and potatoes at a highway roadhouse. They never acknowledged the food, either by words or attention. And the subtle delights of the food were interrupted by a jarring question about court jurisdiction.

I listened and answered with tense impatience and a senseless resistance to the general mood. I could not think my own thoughts, could not escape, could not be myself even for a moment. My role was simply to sit there with my consciousness rented by the hour, simply sit without owning myself, to pay attention, answer questions, smile and eat my creamy dessert.

When the day at the office ended, I drove home to my

apartment house. I stepped out of the elevator at the eighth floor, and walked swiftly down the modernistic, carpeted corridor past a long line of identical doors to my own apartment. I opened the door and felt the cool, dry, air-conditioned air and the silent neatness. The hard, hot Washington day pulsing with government business, throbbing with urgent, important matters, was over. The door closed with a metallic click.

The first thing that greeted me was a feeling of personal emptiness. The apartment was an "efficiency," with a single large room for living and sleeping and a kitchen built into one wall. Large windows looked out over other portions of the apartment house to a narrow strip of trees and to an identical white apartment house beyond. The cool was a relief from the unhealthy heat outside. My suit made me feel constrained and unnatural; I quickly changed to more comfortable clothes and sat down in a chair with a view out the window.

At the office, with the phone ringing, the typewriters clicking, everyone in a hurry, there was no time to feel depressed. But in the apartment everything was absolutely motionless: some very austere furniture, the lifeless view out the windows, and silence.

I was often invited to eat downtown with one or two of the men who happened to be working late, but I usually declined. They would head for a place such as the Rib Room, and the firm would pay. But to me the slow pace of the meal, the Washington talk, and the downtown atmosphere would have been a continuation of my working day. I was impatient to be home and to possess myself and my evening.

I lived at the Wilshire Crescent on Connecticut Avenue in a section of the city that was residential without yet being suburban. The apartment house was modern glass and brick, intended for single occupants. There was no contact between any of the residents except for an occasional encounter, perhaps in the basement laundry room. Going up in the elevator with a couple of fussily dressed middle-aged women with Southern accents, who were carrying their grocery bags, I shrank back.

Most of the occupants of the apartment house (ranging from people in their thirties up to middle-age) seemed to lead conservative lives. Most were women. They were dowdy, perfumed, and deliberate, with faces and expressions that seemed blank and were infuriating to me. I hated to encounter them; I refused even a nod of recognition to those who lived just down the hall, I fled if I was surprised by one of them in the closet-like incinerator room, where I sometimes surreptitiously read the comics in other people's discarded newspapers.

What was I doing leading a life alongside people like this? I was young and full of energy and yet it was as if I was living in an old people's home, shopping and carrying home groceries, eating solitary meals. Shouldn't I be out having adventures, going to parties? It was so horrible to feel old when I was young.

I had briefly tried living with a group of young professional men in a house they had rented in Georgetown. But I felt I needed a shelter. I needed to have my life in perfect order, to go to sleep before eleven, to sleep in a narrow bed (not once in my life had I ever slept next to another person), to be free of the disturbing proximity of people whose lives were beyond mine. It was not that I was old, it was more that I was a tense and frightened child who needed a bedroom sanctuary after being big all day.

Several floors below, among the rows of picture windows that were visible on the arm of the building that I could see, it was possible to watch other residents. I would see one or two lonely women sitting, looking out of separate windows of separate apartments. Another woman might be watching television. A man might be eating a dinner he had cooked. The knowledge that each apartment was similar to mine oppressed me. I liked houses with angles, bays, and turrets—crannies for the soul to hide in, a friend once said. From somewhere nearby, through the walls or the floor, would come an occasional stabbing noise of a record player or radio playing synthetically lighthearted music. Every tiny sound invaded my sanctuary. Unseen faucets turned on and off, and unseen hangers scraped in nearby closets. Dishes were washed next door at a presumably identical sink. I rebelled against going through the same motions in tandem with another person. To hear an unseen neighbor brushing her teeth and know that she can hear you too is somehow a profound exposure of one's loneliness.

Usually I would start some nondescript food cooking and put on some music. Earlier in my life I had passionately loved classical music. Now I played it, but listened little. The truth was that nothing whatever in the apartment interested me. The food I cooked did not interest me, I paid no attention to the music, there was no book or magazine I wanted to read. The only thing I might have attempted was the laundry, but that was only one day out of seven.

I sat in the chair by the window, my mind searching for something to do. I looked over at the phone, the only thing in the apartment that seemed alive. What I kept hoping for was that something from outside would arrive to make life exciting—a letter, a phone call, a new person. But I realized that in truth nothing would happen: the apartment house was constructed against it. I was eight floors above the street. A sign in the lobby warned that ALL GUESTS MUST BE ANNOUNCED. Deliveries and mailmen got only to the downstairs lobby. Each apartment door had a one-way peephole to check visitors. And my apartment was designed exactly for one person's needs.

I got up, stood indecisively, and sat down again. I didn't feel like reading. I felt like doing something with my hands and my strength. But the apartment was constructed against activity. Venetian blinds needed no care, the mail chute was but a step away, garbage vanished down an incinerator chute. Again I looked over at the phone.

There was nothing that I wanted to do that represented a true part of me. I had no interests or hobbies or pleasures that genuinely could be called expressions of myself. It did not really matter whether I stayed in the apartment or walked down to the shopping center or called up a friend or visited a married couple I knew or called a woman for a date. All of these would be as far from myself as just staying at the office. The truth was that there were parts of me I had left behind somewhere.

The intense depression that always hovered over my life, that could be held at bay by activity and outwardness, now took possession of me in an overwhelming rush. I wobbled and the apartment became surreal. Nothing stood ready to respond or join forces. I pitched. I could find no resources within myself. I held tight to the arms of the chair. A hollowness grew within me.

I held tight, and the moment passed. There were a

dozen remedies I could take. I could go to see friends. I could take my car to be greased. I could go back to the office and resume the work that was there to be done. But I refused to let the evening go for things so mundane. It was only seven-thirty, and it was a beautiful night for walking. Suddenly the apartment's sterility became unbearable. I stood for a long thirty seconds, stepped out into the lengthy corridor, slammed the door behind me, ran down eight flights of stairs, rushed through the lobby, pushed open the glass doors, and emerged into the humid evening.

I started walking toward the stores. The supermarket was six blocks off; sometimes ladies returned pushing shopping carts the entire distance. I passed other apartment houses, crossed a large intersection, and reached an Esso station. It had good smells and good associations. I liked the pungent smell of gasoline and the smell of tires. I thought of long trips with my car, the surge and the rhythm of driving especially at night on unfamiliar highways, brief stops at turnpike gas stations in the blazing sun, checking the tires outside the motel on a fresh morning, something going wrong with the car and the satisfying feeling of successfully getting it fixed. The gasoline smelled like outboard motors, lakes and summertime without city staleness. The Esso sign had the look of bright contemporary art against the evening sky.

Beyond the gas station were stores and restaurants. I strolled alone, a little slower now. Here was my Chinese hand laundry. Next door was the dry cleaners. I passed a gift shop, cluttered with pastel cards and other banalities; I thought of the euphemistically named Home for Incurables up one of the side streets and of the sentimental cards that were probably sent there.

I passed a steak restaurant, tangy but without distinction in its customers or steaks, open late for dancing in a darkened, smoky room. Then the movie theater, which usually had Hollywood musicals for long engagements. Another restaurant, this one French and popular with the "girls" from the apartment houses when they went out together. The cooking was rather good (their best dish was veal scallopini) but the restaurant had skimpy tables, tearoom-style waitresses and an atmosphere of sadness. Beyond this restaurant was an upstairs dance studio where moving shadows were seen against the discreetly shaded windows—a place that raised hopes in people to "make new friends." Next came an automatic laundry, and finally a mom-and-pop liquor store, open late with only the middle-aged owners waiting inside.

I arrived at the large, modern, brightly lit supermarket, one of the prime objectives of my tour—although there was nothing I wanted to buy. I liked to walk along the rows of meats and fruits and vegetables, admiring turnips, eggplants, and other things in from the farm. Heaps of onions and potatoes. Exotic frozen foods. The array of canned soups, including such unchanging verities as plain chicken broth (reminder of a day at home with a cold) and beef and noodle soup. Powdered mashed potatoes, the companion of overnight camping trips. Sliced almonds, to be mixed with string beans for a fancy dinner. Leaving the store, feeling revived, I passed the supermarket's parking lot, which was always in a state of marvelous impasse as cars tried to back out and would-be parkers angrily waited for each other.

On the other side of the parking lot was a branch public library. Looking for something that would extend my newly lifted mood, I walked into the library. The main room had modern wooden tables and bright lighting. Some high school boys and girls, mostly in couples, were studying; there were also some older men and women, sitting separately. Here and there was a face, young or old, with something interesting about it. There were a few glances toward me, and reading was resumed. I wandered over to look at the books. Reading had once been an important part of my life, but since coming to Washington I had found it harder and harder to read anything at all. I moved restlessly along the shelves, feeling that I must have read all the good books already; how could I be sure that the others were really worth my time?

In the next aisle I noticed a girl, about eighteen or nineteen, sweet smelling even from where I was, simply and trimly dressed. She was the opposite of the frumpy apartment-house ladies with her bare legs and shining, long hair and her calm, quiet presence. I could have stood beside her, almost touching, not moving as I felt her warmth—a long delicious moment, until she picked out a book and moved away. A shadow passed over me; I walked out without finding a book.

The first major project for myself was my work. Living as an independent person in a city was the second. But the latter was proving to be very hard. In school, friends had seemingly been furnished for me—roommates who were assigned along with a room, or co-members of the law journal staff. The part of myself who lived alone in the city seemed a far cry from my working self, the well-liked daytime person who had many friends. I called on the working self for aid.

I tried to make my work an education and a base for growth in whatever way I could. One of the few ways in which I was able to be creative was through forming acquaintanceships with some of the interesting people who inhabited Washington. I wanted to learn from them, and since no one else seemed to want what I wanted, it was easy. I had lunch with all kinds of Washington people—some my age, some elder statesmen, congressmen, commissioners, lawyers. For me it was a live version of history, and I promised myself to make good use of it when I became a teacher.

Work gave me access to the homes of many married people, and I tried to use this as a bridge from the security of my working self to the far more uncertain person living alone. Married people, both those who were law school contemporaries and older families who provided a sense of substitute homelife, became a staple of my existence. Often these married people provided a real sense of friendship and enjoyment. I even joined in mowing the lawn or raking leaves. But when I tried to use these families as a substitute for deeper needs within me, and visited them out of a sense of my own emptiness, I would usually find temporary comfort but a larger unsatisfied feeling. I will take you on a visit to an imaginary couple a bit older than myself, the Farrells, who lived in a big wooden house surrounded by trees in the Cleveland Park section up the hill from Connecticut Avenue where I lived. They were the kind of people I thought I ought to become—successful, socially competent, and married with young children. Of all the people I knew in Washington, couples like these gave me the most social confidence, because they knew me first and foremost as a former Supreme Court law clerk and a bright young lawyer —a person they readily accepted as one of their own.

I would often call up married friends when I was feeling desperately lonely, maybe after dinner on a weekday evening. In the drugstore near my apartment I might have gone to a phone booth and dialed the number of the Farrells. Martha Farrell answered and sounded delighted. She asked me to hold on a minute, and then came back to the phone, saying, "We're just finishing dinner, and Henry and I would love to have you come on over for coffee." I hung up and with a spring in my step started to climb the hill.

I hesitated at the door, feeling that I had come too quickly, then entered, shook hands with Henry and Martha, and joined them at the antique dining-room table, where they had been sitting having dessert. The tablewear gleamed. "You should have come for dinner," said Martha. "We had a roast that was much too big, and you know we don't need any notice. Won't you have some, I can get it in a jiffy." I hastily shook my head, and Henry humorously interposed, "He's probably just had roast beef at the Rib Room at the office's expense. Come on, have some coffee and dessert."

Henry and Martha were a handsome couple. Henry was tall with horn-rimmed glasses and the air of having gone to good schools and having been part of the successful inner circles there. Martha was also tall and had good looks augmented by good taste—the kind of person who sent homemade Christmas cards. They were unmistakenly an Ivy League couple, and their faces shone with intelligence. They were energetic and athletic, and found life exciting and challenging.

The coffee was excellent, and sitting there, I was conscious of their good taste in general. There was not a banal item in the house, nor was there the Danish furniture look; everything was subdued, individual, original, with some striking works of art and one fine comic modern sculpture. The table seated eight, just right for a Saturday evening dinner party. The house spoke of reading, good music, a varied circle of friends, of art and design.

The conversation was interrupted by the appearance of the children. Henry and Martha's attention switched; now they were full of concern. Their reaction to their children was immediate.

I felt jealous. Neither Henry nor Martha was available for closeness to me nor I to them in any real emotional sense. I could not hug them or touch them or show any affection. I could not tell them my deepest feelings, and they would never tell me theirs. I could not have a separate relationship with either of them. I could not laugh and be playful with them.

"You like bourbon," said Henry as the three adults settled down in the living room. I wasn't much of an after-dinner drinker, but I wanted very much to be sociable, and drinks were part of the Farrells' hospitality. "You've come at just the right time," Martha said when we all were sitting down. "How do you explain what's just happened in the Senate? You're the expert—what do you make of it?" Henry and Martha were deeply concerned about public affairs. Now they were prepared to give their guest full attention. I took the cue gladly, wanting to "earn" my place among them in their living room.

Martha and Henry were genuinely interested. They liked to put an edge on the discussion by occasionally playing devil's advocate, interrupting with humorous sallies, or otherwise reserving a degree of skepticism. In the Farrells' circle, the conversational coin of exchange usually included a soupçon of one-upmanship (I might say something about political power groups and they would, instead of agreeing or disagreeing, ask "Have you read Perroux's *Partisans of Power?*") and also a bit of "deflating." Henry and Martha, and most of their friends, thought "deflating" was a sort of civic duty, beneficial to the deflated person and to be taken by him with appreciative good humor. I found that these thrusts slightly nettled me; my expansiveness was fragile, and I was easily pushed back into myself, but I considered this a weakness I should rise above. I tried to remember that the pokes were good for me.

I thrust into the conversation with new energy, but it refused to take off. Henry was above all a reasonable man. He could make extremes disappear, violent emotions seem more moderate, irreconcilable contradictions seem capable of reconciliation. He could reduce a confrontation of principle to a difference of fact; he could show that no one had enough facts to hold a definite opinion; he could show that one must take a provisional rather than an absolute stand. Henry blunted the edges of things; they lost their capacity for flight. I chewed the ice in my drink.

Suddenly I was restless and bored. I had eaten too many potato chips and peanuts, two items which I hated on principle and also on grounds of how they tasted. Perhaps I understood the sources of the conversation too well. The three of us came from the same backgrounds, had undergone the same schooling. We were liberal, tolerant; we thought about what we were going to say before we said it; we recognized our own limits of competence. We wanted to be a certain kind of person—to be civilized.

I felt angry at my confinement in the living room. Outside was the exciting, liquid night. I missed the supermarket, the drugstore, the public library, all those places and sights that aroused my consciousness. I missed the experience of exploration and adventure. Why had my determination to possess the evening for myself failed?

Remembering, then, the hollow emptiness that had sent me up the street toward the Farrells, I made one last effort to reach out for what I had really come for. I tried to say some things that would please them, to turn them toward me; at the same time the tenor of my voice made an appeal. I wanted to be warmed, to feel a radiation, to unthaw, to feel vibrations, to restore my wholeness. But my appeal (phrased as a compliment to them) was turned aside by depreciatory irony.

I wondered why I had come to see the Farrells. This business of seeing people. "When are you coming again?" they would ask. What, after all, could I be for them? They were a close family; I was a single friend, a separate person. Soon I was leaving, all smiles and thanks, the Farrells were protesting, and Martha was insisting that I come in time for dinner next visit.

One of the greatest of my friendships was with Justice William O. Douglas. It was a unique and special relationship that continued for more than twenty years into the Justice's retirement. I had met Justice Douglas while working at the Court, and the attraction to him was immediate and overwhelmingly powerful. He stood out among the bland figures of Washington like a sun among plastic reflectors. He seemed like a person from the wilds while others came from a habitat of cocktail lounges. His icy blue eyes and rugged face spoke of mountains and clear cold streams. I felt a tremendous desire to become his friend and literally threw myself in his path. My persistence won out.

In a very different way William O. Douglas was as

much a figure of towering greatness as Justice Black. I would have breakfast on Sunday morning and then would phone over to the Douglases; when I heard his voice come on, it sent my pulse rate up. "Want to go for a walk, Charlie?"—those were the magic words. In an hour we would be walking together along the C & O Canal towpath; the Justice's step, quick, impatient, never pausing; both of us propelled by his energy. He was the most exciting, electrifying person, old or young, that I had ever known. His mind was so quick, his knowledge so vast and so detailed, his scope so great—from botany to the government of the Philippines, from stories about playing poker with President Roosevelt to the most advanced theories about ecology, from understanding Washington bureaucracy to understanding the Western antelope—that you had to be 100 percent there to keep up, just as you had to step lively to keep up with his hiking pace.

Both from the Justice himself and the long, hard and physically satisfying walks—sometimes in the snow, sometimes in the heat, sometimes in the rain—I got a sense of renewal. Twenty miles brought out the feeling of having a body again, not just a mind and a suit. As we swung along next to the Potomac River, he would talk and I would listen intently. He knew thousands of people, from cowboys to New Dealers to conservative businessmen, and he had remarkable insights into people—their weaknesses and points of greatness. Those long miles were not always through areas of natural beauty, but we made them beautiful with our energy and our sharing of faith in a better world.

My friendship with Justice Douglas was a most mysterious and extraordinary one. He never made inquiries into my personal life—who my friends were, whether I had a woman friend, what my family was like. At the same time I felt he was extremely loyal and devoted to me, that he would have done anything for me if I needed it, and would always have praised me to others. He talked with great freedom about anything and everything. I often felt that my company was a welcome relief from his official rounds and endless public visitors.

My admiration for Justice Douglas did not blind me to the fact that our relationship was unequal. He could be totally insensitive to someone else's feelings—childish, impatient, inconsiderate, angry, selfish. Compared to his treatment of others, he treated me well. Perhaps I instinctively recognized all of his flaws as like parts of the bad, destructive child inside myself, saw that his loneliness was ultimately similar to mine, and I was more, rather than less, his friend because I knew how isolated he really was. And so I could allow him his full greatness.

Justice Douglas was the Sun God himself, radiating energy in all directions. He was the traveler, the ultimate explorer; he would go farther to the edges of the universe than all but a few individuals could go. He cared not a bit for manners, convention, amenities. Sometimes we would pause, drenched with sweat or rain, for a short rest and a sandwich. Then I could meditate about our wondrous companionship. Just as I knew my time with Justice Black was magical, so I knew those long Sunday walks with Bill Douglas were an ultimate experience; it was being on the knife-edge peak of a mountain summit in the West, the icy wind blowing, snowfields below, the view a hundred miles in every direction, nothing above but limitless sky.

The Sunday mornings when I walked the canal with Bill Douglas were times of new space and magic. But most of the time I experienced my world in Washington, D.C., as a prison of loneliness and exile. In New York, I always found I could relieve my inner misery by walking in the city. I tried to do this with Washington: going to the theater, to concerts, to films, to restaurants, to parks, to sports events, to new neighborhoods, to art galleries and night clubs where jazz was played. But Washington failed to give me what New York had provided. The city was nothing but a larger projection of the sterile working world.

Connecticut Avenue, in front of my apartment house, was one of the main thoroughfares of the city—wide, uncluttered and swift, with few pedestrians but a constant, restless sweep of cars. For two miles in either direction it was lined with apartment houses, relieved occasionally by groups of stores. Some of the apartment houses were modern and huge; others, such as those directly opposite, were much older and held mostly permanent, often elderly, tenants. The side streets had individual homes, closely jammed together nearer the avenue, but farther apart when further away from it. The plainer houses near the avenue usually had older couples, often long-time government employees. The finer homes had well-off professional families, with children and landscaped yards. Most of the city was a vast area of poverty and the desolation of endless white-collar houses. Glistening in the center of the city was the place where "news" happened—the island of statesmen, diplomats, lawyers and black official limousines. Thus the city put its inhabitants into classifications: the glamorous, fortunate, and important; the comfortable middle class; the single, and the poor.

On weekend mornings, the classification system could be felt most strongly. The people in homes with spacious lawns washed cars, mowed the grass, watched their children shoot baskets in the driveway, or breakfasted on warm terraces. I found it hard to wash my car because it had to be parked far off on a side street, away from the avenue's rush-hour no-standing regulations and away from any source of soap and water. I would have been welcome to bring my car to any of a dozen friends' houses, but due to my pride I painfully but stubbornly refused. People who lived in apartments had to find some way to get out on weekends. If they had a car, they drove it; if they had none, they took a bus, waiting a long time for it on an empty corner of the long avenue in the bright sterile sunlight. If the apartment dwellers were old, they stayed indoors. The weekend streets were stale, airless, and deserted.

I realized that Washington was a city of loneliness. There were retired older people alone in small apartments, suffering the pains and fears of illness, finding it harder and harder to go to the store. There were women in their thirties and forties who were unmarried, bitter and lonely. There were all those men in their shirt-sleeves at government jobs. There were all those faintly disillusioned wives of successful men. And because of the invisible barriers of our world, we were as strangers to one another.

In my working life I saw myself as a confident, busy young man, but back at my apartment I was more likely to identify my situation with that of a single woman who had not successfully made it into the circle of family comfort and warmth.

For a young woman coming to Washington after graduating from high school—often in a small town, often in the South—the first step might be a women's residence hotel, perhaps on Sixteenth Street, filled with other young women and a housemother. The woman would get a government job and begin to meet young men, sometimes at the office, sometimes in the jukebox mixer room of her own hotel. Soon she and two or three other women would find an apartment—in a big apartment house if they were not too daring, or on a picturesque street in Georgetown if they were spirited—and commence a few years of being part of the young set of the city.

Life bloomed, but somehow it had no real freshness. If a woman did not marry (and a large proportion did not) she began one day to look at the classified ads in the *Post* and *Star* for modern air-conditioned living quarters—efficiencies or one-bedroom size—in such buildings as Roanoke House, Park Terrace, Potomac Vista, all of them enormous apartment houses along the major northwest avenues or in Arlington, with secretarial service at the front desk, laundry rooms, and underground parking at an extra charge. Dates would be less frequent after this move, dinners with other women at a restaurant more common.

They grew old along with their apartment houses. They became the fussy ladies one saw at the prescription counters of small neighborhood drugstores, buying pills for their chronic complaints. They were seen eating alone, querulously or impetuously, in the nearby restaurants. In their apartments, the clutter and mustiness of the furnishings contrasted with the smooth white walls.

When you feel bad about yourself and your life, there is nothing to do and nowhere to go: you have no power to be happy. I have had this feeling in New Haven and in San Francisco and in many other times and places, but never more so than in Washington. I felt as if I were left out of other people's happiness, that I was melancholy and unattractive while others were sensual, magical, funny, and strong. I was desperately off-center, peering enviously through the window panes of other people's lives. I could visit another lonely person, but we could not share our separate exiles. To me, my unhappiness was a sign of failure and a lack of power, and I was ashamed of this and needed to hide it. Far within I often felt panic that I could never be happy.

In these depressed moods I found not only my world, but the entire city, to be a source of constant unhappiness. Washington was a city with almost no authenticity. The dominant factor was the vast bureaucracy. Bureaucracy encourages docility, acceptance of a dreary life, and a lack of energy or pride. It never pays to work hard or be creative in a bureaucracy—it simply rocks the boat, and there is just as much work the next day. So bureaucrats learn to stretch out their coffee breaks and slow down their work. They learn how not to take responsibility. They shun individuality. The city looked and felt like a place where bureaucrats would live, hoping only to get by.

The second influence on Washington's character came from the fact that it was a center for lobbyists, special interests, and businessmen who wanted favors. This meant a world of phony social interaction. The businessman having lunch with a government official: phony jokes and phony friendship with favors to be asked and awarded as the real but hidden business. What better setting for such encounters than phony restaurants with phony food: phony Italian cooking, phony French, even phony American.

A third influence on Washington was its tourist industry. This was no ordinary tourism but something with a great deal of suffocating hypocrisy as well. For to Washington came all those busses full of high school kids from places like North Carolina and West Virginia and Indiana, groups complete with teachers and steady couples holding hands, to see in person the marvelous shrines of American tradition. And to Washington also came wholesome families. They too sought the American tradition. Washington could not show its real face to these good folk. It could not show its cynicism, its corruption, or its vast indifference. It had to keep up appearances—the whiteness of the Washington Monument, the Capitol Dome, the Supreme Court pillars. For these people, Washington was like an enormous Disneyland before there was a Disneyland. Elderly black men, humble but dignified, guided those endless groups through the hushed corridors of the Supreme Court pointing out that this was where freedom and justice dwelt, just as Disneyland offers the experiences of a nineteenth-century Main Street, U.S.A. How many times I watched those innocent people being shown the same show, believing it all. Sitting in the ornate Supreme Court room while arguments droned on, a high school boy and girl would dare to twine their hands together below the benches where teachers and bailiffs couldn't see. I wondered if they knew that the feeling between those hands was the most real thing in the room, the only thing they should believe in.

There was a quality in the atmosphere which I always felt but never could quite identify. It was the absence of vitality. I used to say to myself that it was a lack of character. If I went to a delicatessen in New York there was a certain energy, a certain sassiness, a certain wise guy quality that gave the place character. The people behind the counter were still in there fighting. When I went to a delicatessen in Washington it simply didn't feel right. I felt that the salespeople in a department store should be angry—angry at working in a department store, at everything from the customers to the goods. In Washington's big department stores, the Hecht Company or Woodward and Lothrop, there was no anger. There was no fight. There was no irony. There was no despair. As long as that fury is there, the person has not given up. It was a sense of total resignation that caused me to feel such overwhelming isolation and despair. Washington made me acutely aware of the deeply spiritual quality of rage.

The city had two seasons. One extended from late fall to early spring. The other was the Heat. Whatever seemed depressing or ugly about the city during cool periods was still something I could cope with, at least on a day-to-day level. But the heat made it seem impossible to exist at all. In Washington, the heat means desolation. Down near the Washington Monument and the Jefferson Memorial the open stretches of grass would be totally deserted, and I felt that any living thing that ventured into the open would be struck down by the relentless sun. The sun's reflection blazed off the white government buildings. To walk across the marble plaza in front of the Supreme Court and up those white steps would be to encounter such an intensity of radiated heat that it seemed as if I could never make it. The heat came down on the Potomac River and made it stink from pollution, so there was no way I could get anywhere near the water without holding my nose. The heat came down on Rock Creek Park and Dumbarton Park, both of which lie in stream valleys, and made them breathless and airless even in the shade of trees. The heat came down on the slums, most of which were formerly handsome one-family houses, and it turned them from places of poverty to places which had the appalling, hopeless lethargy of death. The heat possessed a never-ending power to be worse than I was prepared for. I would come out of an air-cooled building and feel the heat, and I couldn't believe it. Trees turned sickly; birds fell silent.

The oasis of coolness created by air-conditioning made the heat seem more frightening. Looking out my closed window, I felt that if the air-conditioning ever failed I wouldn't survive five minutes. Sometimes I thought of what it might be like in non-air-conditioned hospitals, mental institutions, jails. The thought was too much for me, too frightening to allow. The heat itself seemed the ultimate prison. There was no way out except temporary escape into an artificially cooled building. The stale, sickly deadness smothered all energy, all joy, all sexual feeling, all human concern, all love, all dreams. The cool snow-capped mountains, the icy lakes and streams, the north wind and the Adirondacks seemed thousands of miles away in another and unattainable and hopelessly distant universe. I would turn up my air-conditioner to high and stick my nose deep down into the flow of cool air, gasping for breath like a patient in an oxygen tent.

All during my years in Washington I was concerned with the state of my emotional growth, or rather with the lack of it. I felt as if I were still an eleven-year-old boy trying to pose successfully as a confident adult, trying to cope with a world far beyond my capabilities, attempting to have relationships with grown women in their twenties who seemed far beyond me.

The most constant presence in my life was fear and anxiety. I would wake up in the morning and feel the need to clench my fists and clamp my teeth and squeeze my toes together, which sent tension all through my body as waves of fear and worry came over me. The particular things I worried about changed from day to day or hour to hour or week to week but that terrible feeling of dread remained with me almost all the time. I hated that feeling. It made me afraid of living. It made me not want to wake up, not want to go out, not want to come home, not want to go to sleep.

I worried about getting to work on time. I worried about my clothes and my appearance. A tiny slip in a brief I wrote might cause inconceivable disaster. I feared criticism or pressure from the senior partners. A business trip by plane filled me with worry about reservations and hotels and connections. And yet work was the least of my worries. It was in the rest of my life that I was most overwhelmed. I think I feared most the discovery and exposure of my secrets. All of my sexual feelings were repressed into an intense fantasy world that filled me with unsatisfied desire. I imagined that my sexual incompetence would be discovered. I did not want people to know about my loneliness, my desperation. I was overwhelmed with anxiety when I had to make choices. Should I go to New York for the weekend? The question might consume days of worry. Whenever I purchased anything I would be positive I had made a great mistake and not use the thing or even look at it for weeks after I bought it. I constantly imagined that I had various serious illnesses.

As a lawyer I was constantly pressured to perform flawlessly. I was asked to work a tremendously long and taxing week on many different projects with others constantly interfering, and I was supposed to choose every word with perfection, know every conceivable fact, research every available precedent, and never make a single mistake. I lived in a world of loyalty probes and security checks where everyone was under official surveillance. I felt the social world was equally a test of performance every step of the way. I was expected to drive flawlessly, order a drink with perfection, dance gracefully, play softball with great skill. The overriding value of the Washington world was competence.

It was these anxieties, plus my belief that I must get a start on curing my "sickness," that led me to begin full-time psychoanalysis. I thought I knew exactly what my problem was, and the specific kind of help I needed.

I saw my problem with women as being similar to earlier obstacles in my life—like learning to dive and swim underwater or to drive a car. Each of these activities seemed attractive and necessary but frightening to learn. The fear centered upon the key first step. The longer I would wait to take the first step, the more frozen and frightened I would become, and if I stood there long enough, I would have to give up and wait a few minutes before trying again. But once I had started, I moved along quite well, so that people would often say—what's the problem? You're doing fine. They simply didn't understand the way I would freeze at the beginning.

Any of these problems would be immensely aggravated by the self-consciousness produced when people were watching. It was ten times as hard if someone were idly observing the show. So the whole idea would be to do the thing first in private. But what I couldn't do in private was be competent with a woman because *she* was the audience, the observer. There was no way to practice alone.

More than once I had overcome a fear of this sort by getting a very understanding teacher on my side. If the teacher was the least bit in a hurry or inclined to laugh at me or belittle my fears, it wouldn't work. But if the teacher was really patient and gentle, he or she could help. This is how I viewed psychoanalysis. I would find a reassuring man to teach me about women.

But there was a further problem that did not resemble my childhood fears in the least. Whenever I began to get close to an available woman and she began to take a positive interest in me, there would be an abrupt change in my feelings. Suddenly I couldn't even look at her. I couldn't stand to be with her. I was repelled by her every word, gesture, even by her smell. The change from attraction to total repulsion was so sudden that it was like an iron gate crashing down. After that happened, there was nothing more I could do but look for somebody new.

I felt that this happened because I was a secret homosexual. It never occurred to me that I might be afraid of closeness itself, rather than closeness with a particular sex. Since I had no sexual experiences with men either, I did not realize that my feelings for them could switch off too. I was convinced that if I became less frightened of women, the attraction to men (like other childhood yearnings) would gradually disappear.

Ever since I was eleven years old, I had had strong erotic fantasies concerning boys. The first objects of these fantasies were classmates at school. In all the years from age eleven on, I had never acted out any of these fantasies, but every now and then I had a friendship where there was a secret erotic element carefully concealed from the friend. Why these fifteen years of total repression? I simply felt that my secret was incredibly shameful. In all those years, I never dared tell a single human being about my feelings.

I was sure that anyone I told would be horrified and disgusted. Certainly in all those years I never met a person who gave me the slightest encouragement to think otherwise. I knew, of course, that my feelings were "homosexual" because I had secretly looked at enough books to discover that. Every book about normal sex had some hideous chapter near the back where perversions were discussed. I also knew, although very dimly, that there was some sort of homosexual underground world, but I imagined those inhabiting it to be evil and weird, talking in affected ways, mincing and effeminate and grabbing at people who came their way. I wanted no part of this grotesque and sick world. I did not want to mince and wear perfume and call people darling. It seemed utterly horrible. I wanted to be a strong and independent man. I dreamed of being a leader. I envied athletes. And so to me, my homosexual feelings were something to be hated and overcome, and I felt sure that this could only be done by finding a more "grown-up" outlet with women.

I found a psychoanalyst in Washington and saw him five hours a week, eleven months a year, for five years. A strange feature of my psychoanalysis was that I felt desperately anxious that it be kept a secret from everyone. It seemed a disgrace, and I was always terrified that someone would inadvertently find out. For years I scheduled it at such an early hour that no one would see me come or go.

I felt that I did an outstanding job as the subject of an analysis. I carefully remembered my dreams, wrote them down and brought them in. I did a lot of recalling of childhood and the past. I often analyzed my own experiences and feelings with what I thought was a high degree of perception and intelligence. I never missed a session, never was late, never failed to pay a bill. I told my analyst my negative feelings about him but always protected him from being hurt by telling him that I realized these negative feelings were part of my problem. I loyally stuck it out for five years even though there was little real-life progress. I treated his comments, which were few, with great respect. I always behaved perfectly. Whenever the subject was erotic and sexual, I felt that his comments were stiff and uncomfortable, as if he could barely bring himself to speak on these subjects. He would say something like, "Now this young fellow about whom you had the fantasy. . . ." We both agreed that my fantasies about boys were a form of immaturity, an undesirable carry-over of boyhood feelings. A recurrence was simply a regression on my part, a sign of unfortunate relapse. I did not talk about these feelings as if they had any positive value whatever. I did not think of them as a form, even if undesirable, of love. I did not think of sensuality as if it had any value for its own sake. My feelings were something unfortunate to be overcome.

On the subject of women, I tried to tell myself that if a woman was "suitable"—intelligent, well-educated, pleasant, nice-looking, and well thought of by people who met her—then I ought to be attracted to her. Never once did I explore the idea that there ought to be an element of magic or a true feeling of friendship. Once again I thought the doctor was uncomfortable in the area of sex; he might ask if I were afraid of a woman's "genitals," but I thought he used that word so that it sounded like a specimen under alcohol in a bottle, not something that in any way could be associated with warm desire. If I lost interest in a woman who sounded otherwise presentable, I always felt it was another retreat and failure on my part.

In all of our five years, I never really talked about such things as sharing, love, intimacy, growth, or relationships. The whole positive side of why two people might be drawn together out of shared feelings and love was never discussed. It was an antiseptic five years.

My certainty that I fully understood my own problem and could clearly tell a psychiatrist exactly what help I needed led me to keep control over the whole five years of psychoanalysis, and perhaps my doctor became the victim of my deep and elaborate scheme for protecting myself. I asked him to be my gym teacher, my coach, to put me through the trials of manhood. I did not clearly show him my lack of convincing desire, nor the stubborn, willful, hurt child who kept furiously saying "No." I did not accept my real desires as the truth. I never admitted that I had no idea what sex really was. I had entirely separate ideas in my head concerning "love" (which I imagined as commitment and devotion), feelings toward women (which I saw as a test I must pass), feelings toward men (which I did not consider to be love at all), and playfulness, sensuality, and touching (which I defined as still another separate category). So I spent hundreds of hours, thousands of dollars, years of my life on a project which I myself helped to defeat by never allowing the truth to speak for itself.

Armed with support from my psychoanalyst for the project of manfully becoming sexually successful with women, I plunged into the social world to meet women, have experiences with them, and eventually find a wife. I ordered myself: Come on, just *do* it. Stop stalling!

At first, before I felt too much self-created pressure, it almost seemed as if loving a woman would just happen naturally and I would suprise myself with how easy it really was. I met a woman I liked a whole lot, a woman nicknamed Toby whose company I really enjoyed. She was the daughter of a well-known Democratic senator, and she had been brought up in the world of official Washington. I was flattered beyond words that she accepted my company. She was tall and vivacious and attractive and happy. I felt very lucky. She knew about all kinds of things that had been left out of my youth but which I now wanted very much to add. She knew about dancing and took me off to places where you could dance to a quiet band, and she was so easy and matter-of-fact with me that I began to feel like a good dancer. She liked small night spots where you could hear good jazz. She knew about ordering crazy cocktails with names I had never heard. She had seen that whole fancy formal Washington celebrity world and it had given her poise and assurance, but she was beyond it. Most important she knew about having fun, she knew about laughing. If I was too backward with her, she leaned over and kissed me. She was above all my very good friend.

Then something changed. Distance grew between us and I didn't know what was happening. To my shock and dismay she married somebody I had never even heard her talk about. It happened very fast, and suddenly she was out of my life.

I don't think that what occured was really very surprising. In fact, it happened several more times: I would meet a woman and we would have good times together, but after a while she would marry somebody else. To any woman of that time I must have seemed a totally discouraging case. When women had grown up and were out of college they expected to get married, and every young man that took them out represented that possibility. When they went out with me, our relationship reached a certain level of friendship which provided regular times to see each other, but did not go beyond that level. It did not go on to intimacy, to sex, or to commitment. I doubt if any of these women realized I had simply reached the limit of what I knew, not what I wanted. If they asked me, I was evasive. I do not know if any of them would have been able to take the lead had I been prepared to talk honestly about my feelings.

I was terrified by the concept of marriage. To begin with, there was a tremendous feeling of being hurried and rushed. It was a competitive market and you had to make a choice quickly, or the woman would marry someone else. It was often said that you had no right to continue a friendship with a single woman if you weren't serious about marrying her, for she would be beyond the marriageable age and turning into an "old maid" by the time she was twenty-five. I had had so little experience with relationships that I honestly didn't know who or what I wanted. There was no one to talk with about relationships. I had this horrible feeling that I would be hurried and rushed and suddenly find myself in the nightmare of walking up the aisle of a church or synagogue to be married forever to a woman who, however nice she might be, was really a stranger—saying "I do" in front of the minister or rabbi and all those relatives, when inside I was screaming out "I don't, I don't, I don't."

But even if it had been the right woman, marriage represented something I couldn't bring myself to do. Marriage meant adopting an entire way of life. It meant perhaps first living in an apartment development in Virginia called Parkfairfax, a depressing and ugly group of buildings next to a freeway and a shopping center. It meant moving in a year or two to an even more suburban area like South Alexandria, where we would buy a house in a development. It meant silverware and expensive furniture. It meant do-it-yourself weekends mowing the lawn or hammering at something in the basement. It meant entertaining other young couples and being entertained by them. It meant me standing in the living room and saying to some other couple: "Let me freshen your drinks."

Marriage meant staying permanently in my present job. It meant children, a concept I was utterly unprepared for. It meant spending all of my time with one person when I had just escaped from my family and desperately needed solitude and privacy, at least part of the time. It meant being "adult," which meant no more hope of excitement, no more fun—a sudden and final leap into middle age. It would have been like a prison sentence, for I would have to agree to live in exile from everything I was or wanted to become.

But I knew firsthand the horrors of being alone. Almost everyone around me was married. Being alone meant eating breakfast alone, having dinner alone, going to movies and restaurants alone, spending long weekends alone, even going on vacation alone. As for other single men, they were as lonely and miserable as I; in no sense were they ready for a friendship with me. They were busy trying to get married, and that is how they wanted to spend their time. Women were either "taken" or not. A friendship with a woman who was "taken" was simply unthinkable. There were no models of happy people who were permanently single. So there was only one acceptable way to exist: married, with a home, and family.

Every person over twenty-five who was not married

was stamped a failure. With a man the failure was less acute. First, because "a man can always get married," and second, because a man with a busy and interesting life supposedly had some compensations, but the mark of failure was there nevertheless. One of my acquaintances for an occasional lunch was a famous and distinguished legal figure who was a bachelor. I never saw him without thinking of him as a failure, an unhappy man whom I did not want to be like. Every teenage boy in high school had a girl, every movie had a romance, every friend kept asking me how my "social life" was going, every married woman had an unmarried woman friend for me to meet.

This structure of life was harshly enforced. I became aware of the fundamental fact of unavailability. People simply were unavailable to me except through the system of marriage or dating. Once a male or female friend was married, you could never expect to spend any time with them again except when accompanied by their spouse. They would always present themselves as a couple, and you would be forced in defense to try to become a couple yourself. There was no way you could ever expect a married person to have a one-to-one relationship or even a one-to-one dinner. Likewise, single people were unavailable except in dating situations.

I felt that spending full time hunting for a mate was a degrading and humiliating experience for men and women. The constant asking of friends for names, keeping lists, checking people off—all of this was a heavy burden. For the whole underlying concept was that you were somehow incomplete as a person, that you were not entitled to respect yourself unless you had a mate. It was almost as if single people had no genuine existence. No matter how inappropriate the woman, no matter how little we could possibly have in common, no matter how ridiculous and undignified it was to sit at a restaurant with someone, desperately searching for scraps of conversation, I believed and everyone else apparently believed that I would be more complete attached to this companion than if I had been home reading a book by myself.

To all of us who were single, Washington was a vast competitive marketplace and our job was to meet a large number of possible candidates and select the best one. It was perfectly all right for me to call up a woman I had never met, tell her my name, and simply say, "So-and-so told me about you and suggested I call." Perhaps I would add the fact that I worked at a prestigious firm. I could never get over that this was all that a woman expected by way of explanation, but invariably it was enough. She would say, "Oh, yes, it would be nice to meet you," and all that would be left to do was to agree on an evening for dinner.

There were three groups of "girls"—as they were referred to. First there were women from middle-class families, educated at Ivy League colleges, who held jobs with some educational status. They were "with the CIA" or were economic analysts in some governmental department or were editors' assistants for a magazine, but they were never secretaries. They lived quite elegantly in threes and fours and gave sophisticated cocktail parties and Sunday brunches for all the young Ivy League lawyers they collectively knew. For a cocktail party, but not for brunch, they half-heartedly invited some other women, and these parties—crowded, high-pitched and competitive—were a prime place to try to meet someone new.

The second and far larger group of women was the

secretaries, who usually only had a high school education or maybe a couple of years of college. They were at a wholly different cultural level, although they also gave parties to which many of us went. These women were friendly and less pretentious, but any dating relationship was heavily shadowed by the differing statuses involved. The chance that an Ivy League lawyer would actually marry one of these women was remote. For the men they represented "something to do"; for the women the men sometimes represented no more than a chance for going to a good restaurant and a good movie.

The third group were the home-grown women who lived with their families in Washington and did not necessarily work. There were two varieties. First, there were the women from aristocratic WASP families who had money and raised horses. They were willing to expand their horizons by going out with a young lawyer, but there was no real exchange. It was trying to spend several hours with a woman when there was very little to say, and it was a relief to take her back to her family mansion. These young ladies banded together to give a gigantic, annual black-tie dance, complete with Meyer Davis' Band, called the "Bachelors and Spinsters Ball." Since I was interested in every possible opportunity to meet people, I found someone to get me on the list. All those women in puffy, frilly, candy-colored ballroom finery! And me in a rented tux.

The other group of home-grown women were Jewish, from well-established families who went to synagogue and expected their daughters to marry a young doctor or lawyer. I was *very* welcome in such a household. The enthusiasm was alarming, then terrifying. I imagined that marriage was in the air before I had done more than step inside the living room to meet the parents. I would spend the whole of one of those first dates trying to make it clear that I wasn't quite ready to marry the woman that instant. I thought that ten minutes after I took a woman like that out on a first date, she would be talking about wedding presents and the fact that she had always dreamed of being married by her uncle who was a rabbi.

The real point of all of these encounters lay in the roles and expectations that came with even the most casual date. Hanging over even the earliest encounter was the universal dictum that every date was an occasion for looking over a prospective husband or wife. So it always came back to the concept of a date as a time for finding out if the other person could pass various aptitude and intelligence tests. First were the questions about family and educational background. Then there were questions about culture. We might talk about a movie we had both seen and then the question for me would be, did the woman show intelligence and perception in discussing the movie? If a woman said something awkward, I froze. If a woman showed that she was an intelligent commentator on public events, I checked that off and went on to something else. Eating in a fine restaurant and going to a foreign film were tests; attending dinner parties with married friends was another excruciating test—how well could the woman handle herself with these sophisticated people? If she could not, I was hot with embarrassment; if she could, the hosts always managed to get me aside and say, "We hope you will give us a chance to see more of Elaine." Secretly I wished I could find out things that I could not ask. Was there any insanity or inherited illness in her family? What sort of a housekeeper would she be? Women seemed to want to know less; it was a man's world.

I really felt that once they knew I was a civilized person with an excellent job, that was almost enough. But the ultimate question for both of us was, is he or she as good as I can do? The older and more desperate one was, the more pressure one felt to answer that question with a yes. And once either party said yes to himself or herself, then it was just a question of "landing" the other person.

I also forced myself into a very definite idea of what the right woman would be like. Instead of imagining a woman who was able to make me feel happy, I began to think in terms of abstract qualities. She must be cultured and well-educated, probably from an Ivy League college. She must dress with simple sophistication. She must enjoy the right restaurants and foreign films. She must be approved of in the married circles whose homes I visited. She must be trim and athletic and like the outdoors. She must have the right values and opinions. She must have no serious faults or blemishes. Looking for the right woman was like looking for the right gift or Christmas card. Some stores had stuff that was just too elaborate and fussy or tacky. These I rejected as bad taste. Other stores had things that seemed mass-produced. They were not special enough for me. In the Georgetown section of Washington, there was a small and expensive shop called Ursell's. It sold gifts like salad bowls and candle holders that were in superb, modern good taste. It had place mats that were simple and subdued but obviously expensive and fine. Its Christmas cards were always a little more special and sophisticated than those of any other store, ones with lithographs of a snowflake or of a reindeer serving cocktails in a modern home. I wanted a woman from Ursell's.

It was virtually impossible for a woman to feel equal

to a man in freedom, self-confidence, power, or sense of purpose. The social system forbade equality. It forced women to give up their dignity because every woman who was single and over twenty-one was considered to be in a state of desperation, no matter how hard she struggled to be autonomous. Most women did not get to travel, to have lunch with interesting people, to hail taxicabs and ride to important meetings. It is painful to write about, but the inequality was real.

I would call for a woman; she would open the front door of her apartment, and right away I would be overwhelmed by what I felt to be her sense of inferiority. She opened the door with the attitude of "here I am, take me wherever you want and decide whether you approve of me or not." Almost every woman was completely passive about where we would go or what we would do. If I tried to find out whether she had been to a certain restaurant or seen a certain film, she wouldn't tell the truth. I might find out only later that she had seen the film once before and didn't like it, or that she hated a certain kind of restaurant.

Once I had a blind date during a week in which I was working hard. We went out to an espresso coffee shop for a while, and then I said I really enjoyed meeting her but it was a midweek working day and time to go home. She looked at me and said, "Well, I guess that takes care of that," meaning: "I guess you've seen enough of me to know I'm not worth your wasting any more time." And she said it in a way that implied, "I think it's quite all right to be businesslike about those things—why waste time when you've made your decision?" I hadn't meant that at all, but I just couldn't stand what she said or the way she said it. Even now, many years later, I wince when I remember that and other similar moments. And of course from that moment on, I couldn't stand to be with her. Today I might know how to deal with something like that, but then I could not.

The most painful thing about being with a woman was that I often felt responsible for her sense of self-worth. I simply couldn't stand this. If for any reason unconnected to her I was feeling irritable or depressed or preoccupied, she would always take it personally. If the day at the office was filled with tension and I could not unwind at dinner with the woman I was with, she would probably believe that her conversation or her very presence were making me uncomfortable. If she cooked Sunday brunch and I was restless because I was dissatisfied with my job, she assumed I disliked the way she cooked scrambled eggs. I felt I had no freedom to feel bad at a time when I really needed to share that feeling with someone.

Our dates took place at restaurants, movie theaters, smoky cocktail lounges or a hotel terrace where we could dance. I never would go to any of these places as part of my regular life. I thoroughly disliked dark, smoky cocktail lounges. I did not even like cocktails, and I did not smoke. These were just places that I endured as somewhere I was supposed to go on a date.

I asked every young bachelor I knew for the names of women he wasn't interested in himself, despite the humiliation and indebtedness I incurred, and despite the unlikelihood that they would ever turn a worthwhile woman over to somebody else. I asked every married couple I knew the same question. They often set me up with women they claimed were "so nice," "so attractive" and "fascinating," but who turned out to be total mismatches. I told everyone

I was available and looking. My brother sent down the names of former Radcliffe women. My mother managed to come up with the names of women in New York. Quite often I would take the long, dreary train ride to New York on a weekend for the sake of meeting a woman, and the situation turned out to be hopeless after three minutes. In Washington there was nothing I wouldn't try. I eagerly went to cocktail parties and forced myself to meet single women and somehow get their names and phone numbers and tell them I would call them up. If I went to an office where there was a pleasant receptionist or secretary, I tried to talk to her while waiting. If I heard that a woman was divorced, I phoned her. I went, God help me, to "young people's events" at the Young Women's Hebrew Association.

This process was like endlessly looking for a job, having unsuccessful interviews, checking the want ads again, feeling an immense drain of energy into a vast project that always hung over me, trudging home after yet another disappointment, and having to start all over again.

All of this pressure, competition, commodity standards, artificiality and pretense furnished the context for my struggle to find and express sexual feelings toward women. Other men at least were propelled by genuine desires, which gave them energy and which a woman could feel, while in my case I tried to pursue women while not feeling desire but hoping to find it. I never dared take a woman into my confidence, never once asked for help, never asked a woman to be on my side, never thought I had a right to. I knew of no easy way to be playful and sensual. I expected mutual desire to leap fullborn from two stiffly polite people who made genteel conversation one minute and then suddenly turned off the lights and began to paw at each other the next. I knew nothing about closeness between people, and thought I had to crash directly into physical intimacy—that my sexual feelings were supposed to arise no matter what the circumstances. I did not even feel permission to do with women what I secretly wanted to do: touch them, whisper to them, be warm without a word spoken. I stared at photographs of beauty queens in the newspaper, trying to imagine how I could find them exciting and attractive, as I assumed all other men did, when all I could see was an artificial empty smile.

But the greatest barrier of all was my belief that sex was simply a matter of "having done it," that once I passed my driver's test I had nothing further to learn and would have no further problems the rest of my life with any woman. I fantasized that a woman, if she found out she was being led along by a man who was inexperienced, would angrily consider her time to have been wasted: "Why are we sitting freezing to death parked at the curb in this car if you don't even know how to drive?"

Despite all of these difficulties I fully expected myself to succeed. Imagine me at a restaurant with a woman named Elaine. After much debate I've picked this restaurant to show that I'm a person of sophisticated taste. It is an expensive small French restaurant near Lafayette Square. I time our arrival so it will be smooth: easy parking and no waiting for a table. I am knowledgeable about what food to order, and command service easily. It is a higher-class restaurant than Elaine is used to, and she is impressed. Then we engage in just the right conversation about the expected topics: politics, my work, music, her background, other restaurants. If I said anything wrong it would be a faux pas, like knocking over a water glass on the table. I would try not to let it happen again, and I would be upset that it did happen. As for showing my real feelings, I believed that this was exactly what I was *not* supposed to do. "Act like an Attractive Person," a voice inside me said. That meant "try to learn to act better than you do. Try to change how you act to conform to the way Attractive People act." And so we smiled and nodded our way through the evening.

We would go up to the woman's apartment, usually in a big modern apartment house. It would be decorated beautifully. She would sit me down on a sofa, put on some soft music, and mix a late-evening drink. Then she would come over and sit next to me. Perhaps I would take off the jacket of my Brooks Brothers suit and sit there in white shirt and tie. For a moment I might show my real feelings, how much I yearned for something besides my present life and job, and she would tell me I ought to do more "interesting" things. Go to Europe on my vacation. Join a play-reading group. Take a summer cottage at Rehoboth Beach. She wanted me to add trappings to my life, but she didn't understand my real sense of longing.

After a while, it would be time for a second drink and for sitting still closer. Her hand might slip into mine and maybe her head would rest on my shoulder, and with my arm around her I would say to myself, "Come on, Charles. This is it. This is what it's supposed to be. Go through with it. This is as good a person as you're going to find. Now it's time for mutual desire. This is right. Do it."

Then all of a sudden I would feel that it was a lie, that I didn't really feel anything, and there would be an awful moment when I would say, "It's really very late, I'd better be getting home." The woman would surely think that in some way she had failed, and I had to make all kinds of fumbling reassurances that she was really great, but this wasn't quite the right time. Beneath those reassurances was a crimson sense of shame that I had lost my courage and failed again. Despite all the reassurances to each other, it would be obvious to both of us that we would not see each other again. She would say, "Yes, it is sort of late," or she might even say, "I hope I'll see you again soon." I would say, "I really like you." Then I would put on my coat, perhaps kiss her good night, and push the elevator button, seeing her for the last time as the steel elevator door shut.

My view of women in the world of Washington was greatly distorted by the view I had concerning myself. I had absolutely no reinforcement to think that the way I really was on the inside would be appreciated by anyone. I thought the more that showed of the real Charles within— that Charles of fears, anxieties, childishness, glee, despair, awkwardness, eagerness, terror—the less acceptable I would appear. I wanted to become a different person— polished, smooth, capable, confident.

I did not think the person within me could be loved by anyone. But I did not expect the new polished person to be loved either, for he was admittedly not lovable, and was not designed to be lovable. He was designed to be attractive— to be what other people approved of. He was designed to catch the approval of important people and friends and that right woman, the woman who would meet with his approval.

Given this view of myself, I was all too ready, consciously and unconsciously, to invite women to be interested in me primarily because of my status and achievements. And women of those times, because of their own upbringing and the social system they found themselves in, may well have been all too ready to deal with me on the terms I offered. Inevitably another part of myself resented women for their willingness to accept my terms, and their failure to see the "real me." I tended to see women as more programmed, more status-oriented, than perhaps many of them really were, even in those days. Certainly it was unfair of me to put all the blame on them. But my resentment had at least one advantage: it enabled me to see the plight of women, if not with sympathy, at least with a detached clarity which ultimately brought forth my compassion.

The happiest relationships I had during these years were with several families and especially with their teenage kids. I never gave myself "credit" for any of these friendships, however. I was supposed to be finding a woman, and anything else seemed at best a diversion. But sometimes I was so starved for companionship that I would forget my self-imposed task.

Whenever I would visit an older married couple, I would also become acquainted with their kids. In the living room there would be talk and drinks with the adults, and I would feel the need to perform, the need to pay attention, but I would be bored. The moment one of the kids entered the room there was a subtle change. I really liked them and showed it. When we talked about something, perhaps a book, politics or school, suddenly I was putting real feeling into the conversation and getting a real response. There was connection which I could not feel with the parents. There was some warmth.

Whenever I could, I would disappear with the family's son down to the finished basement, which was his territory, for a game of ping-pong. The basement felt completely different from upstairs. It was comfortable. Something important happened when we played ping-pong. We had fun. Teenagers always found out certain things about me that their parents never knew. I get really mad when I miss the ball. With a little teasing, I get even madder. Being mad in that way is one of my funny sides. It makes other people laugh and pretty soon it makes me laugh. Down in the basement we laughed a lot, and that never happened upstairs. I like to make faces. I like to show how triumphant I am when I hit a good shot, how superior I can be when I serve an ace, how totally crestfallen I am when I hit the ball into the net. I would put on my serious adult face when we went back upstairs.

It seemed to me that teenagers led a life that I had never known. They had an automobile community that drove around the city on Saturday night. They had their own music, full of their own experiences, not the Mozart and Beethoven I knew in high school. Teenagers were not so burdened with responsibilities and outside concerns as I had been; if they went to a drive-in, their thoughts were dominated by hamburgers and music, not worries about work due for the next day. They didn't merely seek fun, they were fun. They dared each other. They dared themselves. They tried to push each other and themselves into new experiences. They were willing to scare themselves and others, to get into trouble, to push their luck.

These teenagers still had juices running in them. Their bodies were still warm. Their faces could still smile, and they loved freedom. I greatly envied them. But I saw all too clearly that their world did not last. Soon they went off to college and then to law school or medical school. I saw some of them later, and all traces of playfulness were gone.

They had become young adults like myself.

Gradually I got to know one teenager very well, and through him a number of his friends. Dave was just starting high school. He loved to drive around, first in my car and then in his ancient car when he got it. Driving around was always something special. In the first place, unlike anything older people did, it was always unpredictable. I never knew where we were going next, and David simply let the ideas come to him. We might suddenly veer off our route to ring the front door of a friend's house, spend a few minutes, and then zoom away. We might stop unexpectedly for jelly doughnuts. We might suddenly find ourselves at a bowling alley and Dave could try duckpins for twenty minutes. We might find ourselves out in the country. We would be guided by impulse and that made every moment interesting. Dave knew how to make the city into a playground while adults had to follow its commands.

Wherever we went, the radio was always turned on to rock 'n' roll. This music seemed to be invented in the mid-1950's for teenagers like Dave. It sounded completely different from anything I had ever heard. Like Dave, it had energy. It had a beat. It was funny. It had real feeling. It had a kind of freedom which popular music had never known. I liked it from the first time I heard it. It made me feel good.

Dave related to me in a way that no one else in Washington did. He was comical, and he let me be comical. He made faces at me. We made faces at each other. He teased me. He hit me over the head with pillows. He tickled me. He made me be furious in a way that caused us both to break up laughing. He was daring. We were always doing outrageous and slightly illegal things, like drinking beer in the car. He stole the round knob off my gearshift. He conned me into taking him to the movies. He dragged me off to drive-ins and stuffed me full of Mighty Mo Double Hamburgers covered with every form of relish. He introduced me to places that I had never before entered, like pinball arcades. He glamorized my car. He peeled out and left rubber tire marks on the pavement. He taught me how to brake by down-shifting the gears. He would show up at the office in the late afternoon and sit with the receptionist where I could see him, and whenever I would look his way he would elaborately stare at the ceiling, and pretty soon I decided to call it a day and off we went. With every other person I was the serious bright young lawyer, frowning as I gave utterance to some profound thought. If Dave saw that coming, he would put an ice cube down my neck.

My relationship with Dave was part of a perilous gamble. I felt instinctively that the rock 'n' roll culture, despite its commercialism and conformity, had the glimmer of an authentic opening to greater freedom. I risked a loss of identity in order to learn something new. In that tinny-sounding, make-believe place that floated on the energy of the Top Forty I could sometimes experience feelings that had no other means of expression and might otherwise have ceased to be felt or even remembered. If it took the nasal voice of Rick Nelson on 45 r.p.m.'s to preserve in me the faith that I might yet be romantic, it mattered little that the music was meant only to please the jukebox audience.

In the same way, through Dave I preserved at least an intimation of what closeness and sharing felt like. It was a relationship that necessarily carried with it some self-hatred. I gave stature to Dave at the expense of my own stature, rather than as an equal, for I could muster little sense of my own worth. I felt guilt and fear because my repressed and secret homosexual feelings played an essential part in my desire to have a relationship with Dave. Unlike my forced interest in women, I had real sexual feelings for Dave. I desperately hoped that neither he nor anyone else, especially the members of his family, ever suspected. At times I told myself that no one did suspect, and at other times I was overcome with the fear that everyone knew. It would have meant the end of the relationship, I was certain of that. I feared that I was doing something shameful and might be caught.

I let myself see in Dave a degree of autonomy that he did not really possess, for in truth he was just as much a prisoner as I. And I risked and suffered pain when his changes of mood left me temporarily stranded. At the same time, I constantly would promise myself to stop, and resume my real job with women, going out to Georgetown to visit a Radcliffe woman with whom I would discuss the economic situation and the Supreme Court.

What I did not see then, but recognize now, was how much the odds were against all of us in that Washington world. I did not see the struggle that my life really was, for the sources of my frustration and unhappiness seemed so varied, so unconnected, so much the result of my own unique problems, so much the reflection of my own prejudices, that I placed most of the blame for my condition on myself and the remainder on what I saw as the failures of other people.

As it was, I fell into the malaise of a life without hope, a day that was really just filler, an existence that had given up on all possibilities. When I felt that way I just let things go: reading, exercising, walking, discovering. I had a low attention span, low energy, and a low ego. There may have been a dim resistance in me, but I did not have the strength to create anything or enjoy anything.

In Alfred Hitchcock's film *The Lady Vanishes* he uses one device with marvelous effect, although it comes from many older mystery stories. The heroine meets a nice old lady who sits with her on the train and joins her for tea in the dining car. Later the heroine falls asleep, and when she awakens, the lady is gone. The heroine asks the people in the compartment, and everyone smilingly denies that there ever was such a lady. The heroine goes to the dining car, but the waiter smilingly tells her that she had tea alone. Other passengers who were in the dining car shake their heads. None of them saw any nice old lady. The waiter even produces a bill—tea for one. Finally a psychiatrist with a thick accent appears and tells the heroine that she has suffered a hallucination from being overtired and must rest. That is the way I felt in Washington, D.C., in the fifties. Every other person I knew was part of a conspiracy. Senior partners, young lawyers, waiters, and friends all smilingly told me that my feelings were something I had imagined. There was not one scrap of evidence, not even a restaurant check to help me believe they were real.

As I walked back toward my own apartment house after an evening where I had once again failed to break down the walls surrounding my life, I would be overcome with the feeling of not really living, of just marking time. Nothing was happening, nothing would happen. In rage and despair, I rattled the bars of my prison.

When I entered the glass doors of the lobby of my building, I would feel very tired. I had tried as hard as I could to do what I had to do in my world. For this night at least I owed no more to anyone. In the floor-length mirror in the lobby, I caught an image of myself. A young lawyer in a Brooks Brothers suit, shined shoes, and a short haircut. A young man already old, already encased in that suit: stiff, taut, inflexible, frowning—unlovable and unloving.

The Turning

Three

The kids—they found the road again. *We* found it. *All* of us together made a new spirit possible.

I saw new consciousness first in Berkeley, California, in the summer of 1967. I saw it more deeply at Yale, 1967–70. It changed me and changed my life. I remember this as a time of incredible excitement and discovery, of opening up to unknown realms and corridors, lights and colors, undreamed-of places in the mind and the feelings. It had the power of a primal event which had to be accepted with wonder and awe. There was a sense of dawn, of day-break over the land.

Spontaneously, almost accidentally, a large number of people discovered that they could change. They could grow by expanding their minds and opening up to new ways of thinking. Old ways of thinking had become entrenched, obsolete, and finally destructive. A larger vision was necessary. New consciousness was the beginning of a period of profound individual liberation and growth, and it spread the knowledge that such growth is both possible and necessary.

A change in people was the one kind of reform of American society that had never been pursued on a national scale. Political reform, radicalism, or an economic and political revolution—all of these still left people, their values, and their capacity to live together essentially unchanged. But the growth that new consciousness produced demonstrated an ability to change values, goals, priorities, economics, and thus it could fundamentally alter society at the source. It was growth in the species sense, in the sense of evolution.

The important fact of change and growth in people was not easy to see at the time it began. The first waves of change produced a spectacular but transitory new culture, the so-called counterculture, which drew attention away from the underlying process that was creating it. Political confrontations were sometimes effective, sometimes not, but they were often distractions that obscured personal growth. People looked for immediate, simple political results, rather than at the more complex, down-and-up graph of growing. And even the deeper changes were part of a much greater cycle which could not be discerned at the time. The whole process was biological, an experiment by nature.

A crucial phenomenon of this change was opening up, both to an inward universe and to the world outside. People turned away from the pressure to become narrowly adapted to achieving external success and turned toward "the other side"—the immense realm of self-knowledge that modern society had increasingly ignored. Opening up was accompanied by *flow*. Flow meant closeness and sharing between people, greater energy, creativity, music, excitement and motivation, intense feeling, a sense of community. Until we felt ourselves and others flowing, we did not realize how much had been walled off from our lives and from our society.

Growth and change opened people to dimensions of themselves which alienation had banished from awareness. One of the first to be uncovered was the child inside of us, both the naïve, trusting, happy, laughing spirit and the frustrated, angry rebel.

The new consciousness of the late sixties was only a beginning, but it restored direction. It turned us away from sterile corporate materialism, and toward the human cause. It allowed people to feel again the truth of freedom and equality and rebellion. It restored the immensity of spiritual experience. No one at the time could see where the road would lead, what hardships and disappointments it would bring, what countryside it would pass through.

I left Washington, D.C., in 1960 and joined the faculty of Yale Law School in New Haven, Connecticut. Internally I had not changed very much from the young lawyer of the 1950's, but I vastly improved the external conditions of my life and in some ways became a happier person. I had more freedom, and I loved my work. A university was a choice spot in a threatening world. I was free to think and teach, to write, to talk with students, to play any part in the outside world. I may have felt like a misfit in Washington, but I felt ideally suited to the classroom, to being a scholar. I knew that the university was a retreat, but I had had enough of the "real world."

I designed my own courses to emphasize the nature of the American political and economic system that I had experienced firsthand. I wrote articles for law journals and popular magazines. As early as the summer of 1960, before I had even started teaching at Yale, I had imagined writing a book warning about what was happening to America. In very radical terms, I saw the erosion of individual liberties, the growth of arbitrary governmental power, the waste of our resources, the loss of what I considered basic human values in society. My education in Washington, from Justices Black and Douglas to what I had seen as a lawyer, served as background. I was interested in many areas—constitutional law, planning and allocation of resources, welfare, property, criminal law, individual liberty. I wanted to tell people that our system had become so distorted that the very nature of our country was being changed, that whole areas of choice were being closed off.

All of that time I was engaged in a search. I was trying to find a way by which the dangerous trend might be halted, a way to put our society more in touch with the needs of people. Most thinking about government centered on the needs to improve institutions such as the courts, Congress, and the Presidency. I suggested more democratic participation in the bureaucratic process, more firmly established rights for recipients of governmental assistance, strict constitutional limits on the activities of big government, a renewal of the spirit of the Bill of Rights. But such changes did not take place. On the contrary, things continued to get worse. Gradually I began to believe that reforms of the governmental system were not and could not be enough. There would have to be an affirmative flow of new values. There would have to be a counterforce to match the power of the corporate state. I saw the need, but I could not imagine where the new flow of human values would come from.

In Washington, concern for individual human liberty was steadily being eroded, while arbitrary power grew. Both the Kennedy and Johnson administrations stood for greater State power, without in any way seeing that it was crushing individuality. Abroad, the Vietnam war had begun. In the country as a whole, an increasing distortion of priorities led to a loss of beauty and meaning in rural areas and cities, replaced by sterile shopping center service areas and urban decay. Only at Yale did I feel a sense of community and shared purpose as I walked around the peaceful campus.

But increasingly I had the sense of a comfortable imprisonment. New York was only ninety miles away. If I traveled by train, there were foul railroad cars and exasperating, unexplained breakdowns that could at any time trap the passengers within for hours. If I drove along the Connecticut Turnpike, I looked in my rear-view mirror to see gigantic trucks bearing down on me, and I seriously came to believe that I was risking my life in driving the crowded obsolete freeways to New York. And that city, once reached, seemed so harsh, so speeded up, so untrusting, that a day there produced a splitting headache and a deep desire to return as fast as possible to the sanctuary of Yale.

I was ready for something new and rewarding, but I did not know where to find it. In 1966 I started attending undergraduate English classes in my spare time, reading the books and talking with students about them. It felt great. Nobody else in my position did it, but nobody stopped me.

The lesson was clear. Start doing what you want to do. Stop doing what you don't want to do.

I became a part of the changes of the late sixties by a process that at the time seemed uniquely my own, apparently unrelated to the history of many young people who formed the core of the transformation. Later I saw that my own rebellion, my need to change, was much the same as younger peoples', except that in my case I had more experience with living in the corporate state and a far more solid position in that world. But in different ways all of us were victims of society's broken promises, and all of us believed there could be something better.

In the spring of 1967 my dependence on the college campus was so strong that, even though I had my first semester's leave of absence from teaching, I remained on the campus talking with students and working on a future course. But the summer filled me with apprehension. I had tried everything for those lonely months—dude ranches, organized pack trips, visits to family and friends. It was especially frustrating because I felt I should be happiest during the summers, when I was free. This situation led me to spend two months at Berkeley, a college campus with western fresh air and sunshine, in the beginning of the summer of 1967.

My stay in Berkeley was brought about by the initiative of a single individual, Michael Entin. It is of the essence of the 1967 spirit that this sort of positive intervention in another person's life could happen. Michael's barging into my life reflected one of the most important aspects of new consciousness: people took initiatives with other people, even people they hardly knew. People were eager to give, eager to take responsibility, eager to share what they knew.

I was a member of the faculty committee on admissions at Yale Law School, and Michael was sent to be interviewed by me in 1966. I looked at his file and saw that his grades were not high enough for him to get in. So I took him out for tea instead of interviewing him, told him to remain at Berkeley for law school, and wished him much happiness.

A year later I was in Berkeley for a week's visit, expecting nothing but a refreshing change of air. As late as spring 1967 I knew absolutely nothing about hippies or a new consciousness, although the phenomenon had existed in San Francisco for some time. Walking around Berkeley on a Sunday, I was attracted to a big crowd of people in the park near city hall, where some music was about to be played. Suddenly, out of nowhere, Michael came rushing up. He reminded me of our brief meeting in New Haven, and said he was going to law school at Berkeley. Almost in the next breath he was telling me I should stay in Berkeley for the summer, that I could use his apartment because he was temporarily moving to an experimental dormitory, and that he would introduce me to all sorts of new things that were happening.

Of course I refused. I was not prepared to take anything offered so freely. I assumed it was a courteous gesture by someone who was overenthusiastic. A few days later, with stiff and awkward thanks, I returned to a hot and boring New Haven.

In a couple of weeks, Michael phoned me in New Haven and asked what date I'd be arriving and said the apartment was all ready—as if he had never put much stock in my refusals. To my surprise I found myself saying yes, I would come. My back was in bad shape, and I was confined to doing very little. This led me to think of going to Berkeley as a convalescence, and gave me a kind of "permission" to go.

Berkeley had long been known as the nation's most politically liberal and radically activist campus, and it had recently been the subject of intense publicity because of the Free Speech Movement. It had a special aura deriving from the open, easy-going California way of life and the large number of bookstores and coffeehouses that served an intellectual and bohemian population. It was close to Oakland and San Francisco, which from Jack London to the beat generation of the 1950's had the romantic, salty taste of native radicalism. And in 1967, San Francisco, because it was the origin of psychedelic rock music and a focus of hippiedom in the Haight-Ashbury district, became a center of new consciousness. So Berkeley was then a very special place, unique among college campuses. I did not know this, but I soon found out.

Mike's apartment was on Derby Street just east of College Avenue, about a half mile south of the campus of the University of California. It was on the second floor of a two-story building that had been divided into about eight pleasant and reasonably spacious apartments. The bedroom, a small room with large glass panels on two sides, looked out over some flowering trees and shrubs past a couple of nearby buildings and over rooftops to the San Francisco Bay and in the far distance, the Golden Gate Bridge. The kitchen had an equally fine view. A giant L-shaped living room was full of posters and colorful decorations, including a huge bulletin board. That was all, except for a big closet and bathroom. It was cool, bright, and quiet. Mike stopped by frequently, but did so in a way that left me with a feeling of privacy. He wanted me to see and believe that a new world and a new vision were being created in Berkeley.

Outside the apartment there was indeed a new world. It was not bizarre or the least bit strange. The exaggerated stories of hippiedom never seemed real to me. If anything, it was more like a small-town world, or even the still smaller, friendly world of a children's storybook.

If I stood quietly, I could see a lot of things happening on my street. Motorcycles and brightly painted cars and trucks would drive by. Long-haired boys and country-looking girls came and went. Each frame house possessed a unique appearance and personality. Some windows had signs or posters, some hinted at exotic decorations or living arrangements within. I began to enjoy watching these fresh, happy-looking people come and go. Occasionally someone, usually one of the girls, would look directly at me and smile, and I would be flustered, but in a stiff law-professor way might smile back.

People just seemed happy and satisfied in Berkeley. The mailman was not the bitter, cynical, dissatisfied man, ready to pour out grievances if invited, that I would expect to encounter in New Haven. He seemed to enjoy both his job and life in general.

When walking alone in New Haven, I had often been stopped by suspicious police who thought that since I was not walking a dog, I must be a prowler. I even wrote an article about such encounters. In Berkeley you could walk very slowly or stand still or sit down just about anywhere. If people noticed you, they accepted you as a person who was just sitting down on the grass or on a bench or on a sidewalk. I often saw people alone enjoying themselves, playing a guitar, reading, or staring at a tree, a bed of flowers or a view I had never before noticed. I would pause at a corner and see a tree with filmy, dreamy leaves. Or a flowering shrub. One house that held my imagination was an old and almost ramshackle frame house of redwood, with vegetation growing up on all sides of it, and outside stairways, like fire escapes but made of wood, giving it the look of a children's playhouse or a stage set. There was a hint of posters and candles within.

When I started a walk by going down Derby toward Benvenue, music always seemed to come bursting out of windows. The music was 1967 rock: the Beatles' *Sgt. Pepper's Lonely Hearts Club Band, The Doors,* and *Surrealistic Pillow* by the Jefferson Airplane. I listened to high guitar notes, soaring, visionary, making me shiver inside. I would pause and feel how it fitted the scene—the sunny street, the telegraph poles, the bright flowers and foliage. I'd imagine whoever might be inside—a bearded poet sitting on the floor reading Zen philosophy, a long-haired California girl eating fruit and listening to Simon and Garfunkel's *Parsley, Sage, Rosemary and Thyme.* On the way toward the campus I might pass a quiet church and see someone sitting there, just sitting, playing the flute, and playing it so I felt he was saying something about the big trees and the sky beyond.

College Avenue, from Derby Street to the U.C. campus, was lined with family-sized homes and small apartment houses and finally a couple of towering modern dormitories. There was a small gas station, a church or two, and a block-size university playing field built over a parking lot. In the morning a tide ran in the direction of the campus and in the afternoon the flow of people reversed.

Just down the block from where I lived on the west side of College Avenue was a grey frame house I would notice as I walked by; it had an old panel truck parked in front. It was apparent that quite a number of people lived in the house. They were all young, most likely students. Outside there were usually one or two motorcycles, and maybe an old car. Sometimes the panel truck was there, the sort of small truck you see making deliveries of groceries in New York City, maybe from Gristede's, the select grocery store that was part of my childhood. Oh, how dull Gristede's seemed, how like the Sunday duty-bound walk across Central Park for family visits, when I was a child. But this panel truck had entered a new life. It had been reborn.

The kid or kids who owned the truck had painted it and decorated it and taken it out of its Gristede's life, and now I imagined it went to marvelous faraway places, maybe on picnics or camping, with sleeping bags, guitars and knapsacks, with room for sleeping inside and paisley curtains to give a little privacy. With the smell that I later came to recognize as frankincense, and with flowers, words and other decorations painted all over the outside, the whole truck seemed an expression of humor, happiness, high spirits and FREEDOM. That's the word—that truck, with its long-haired, blue-jeaned, knapsacked, funny-hatted, loose, jaunty, happy kids, was something free.

Those kids, living in that grey house (which perhaps was painted inside much like the truck was painted outside), with weird colored lights, mattresses and pillows on the floor, incense, guitars and posters of Allen Ginsberg or Karl Marx or Marlon Brando—those kids, cooking as informally as I might cook over a campfire, probably not worrying about recipes or dishes or too much cleanliness, but moving, swaying, bobbing, dipping to music—when they piled into that truck (an unbelievable number could get into the truck, and their stuff too, and their dogs, not Park Avenue dogs as dull as Eighty-sixth Street, but shaggy hippy dogs, as free as the kids themselves)—those kids, when they took off for someplace, it was surely to a place where I had never been.

There was a feeling of enchantment. I was sitting in a glade of tall redwoods on the campus watching the pattern of shade and sunlight the needles made on the ground. In the middle distance a boy appeared like a woodland faun, a sack over his shoulder, gathering bottles from trash can to trash can for some mysterious purpose. I watched his progress until he saw me. He looked at me, paused and smiled, then waved. And went his way.

Noon in Sproul Plaza became the most exciting and colorful part of my day. The plaza is the midway of Berkeley, a broad walk that starts with the main entrance to the university at Telegraph Avenue and Bancroft Way, and leads past the administration building on the right side and the student union and cafeteria (separated but joined by a covered walkway) on the left. It was thronged with people, coming, going, standing.

Along the wall were set up about one or two dozen small folding card tables at which students sat with signs and literature for various causes. Three or four units of people would be gathered for a heated political discussion or argument. Other, looser groups gathered around musicians—sometimes a guitar player, sometimes a singer, sometimes a small informal country band. The midway was the route of a parade in both directions, of everything from professors and clerical workers to the ultimate in gaudy hippie finery—purple capes, black top hats, beads and medallions. Then there were the people with knapsacks, sleeping bags, and hiking boots, coming, going, sitting for just a moment around the splashing fountain in the center of it all, looking as if they might be headed outward, for remote mountains and lonely beaches.

This place, Sproul Plaza, this time, noon, these days—the sunny clear days of June 1967, with the brisk breeze from the ocean and the brown and green Berkeley hills behind the scene, with redwoods and other trees in the foreground, and the tall Berkeley Campanile off to the right, with occasional noontime rallies and speech-making and Friday rock concerts in the sunken plaza to the left—this place was a center of the hippie-love revolution, the revolution of politics, music, clothes, and attitudes. From here it would spread all over America, to the grimy streets of Eastern cities, the slick covers of *Time* and *Newsweek,* past the negative interpretations of Eastern intellectuals, like a bright swirling bubbling tide of clear fresh ocean.

There were two entrances to the downstairs dining commons, as it was called, with red, amber, or green lights indicating if there was a long or short wait in line for lunch. I'd go sit at my favorite lunchtime table which was in the center of everything, facing the big high windows and the people. Most of the young people were outside eating oranges and yogurt, while the cafeteria was full of lady clerical workers who ate salads, and men in white shirts with no jackets, and perhaps a few students. I sat at my table, which could have been in the Department of Health, Education and Welfare in Washington, or in University Hospital in Boston, or in the student union at Eugene, Oregon, or in a large office building in New York—but no, something was different.

In all of those other places I have mentioned there was

only one possible reality outside. In Washington there were the halls, the Civil Service regulations, the gradations of employment, G-6 or G-14, the color photographs of the President, the loyalty-investigation system, the system of personal evaluation and promotion, the buses lined up to take workers home at four or four-thirty in the afternoon.

Here I might have felt the large institution surrounding me, the hierarchy of faculty and staff, the isolation of my own life. But instead, I felt myself in a very changed reality. Much of that feeling came from what was actually outside: California, the redwoods, a stream flowing in a small ravine. And upstairs in the plaza was the carnival of life I have already described. But my feelings were even more changed than these externals could explain. There was some deeper transformation.

I felt I was neither bored nor restless nor lonely, but living in a new kind of community, a center of life. There was everything here that is needed at such a center: books and bookstores, coffeehouses and small Chinese and Mexican and other places to eat, lawns and walks and benches, playing fields and tennis courts. There was music and political talk and mysticism and religious talk, and love of nature. And surrounding the plaza and beyond the campus, nestled within the larger environs of the sea and mountains, was a community to live together in. Beyond were beaches and mountains. The Bay and its great bridges. The excitement of driving across them. The marvelous city of San Francisco —not a city at all, but a place of magic with exotic restaurants and magnificent views and the fog coming in, and fog hanging over the Marin hills and trails on those hills and kids hiking those trails and campfires lit at night and guitars being played around them.

And so the cafeteria might be a spaceship. It represented the possibility that there could be a new reality within a physically unchanged America. If people changed, if one's mind changed, somehow it could all be different. I did not understand it, but I felt it. The cafeteria-spaceship might once have been docked in Boston or Washington, D.C. But now it had flown out here, and the reality that formerly had been outside was left behind, and the spaceship had landed in a new and beautiful place, and I could walk out of the cafeteria at any time and be in a new world.

Back up in Sproul Plaza, someone might be playing the guitar and singing, and there would be a crowd gathered around. The songs were popular folk songs. There was a lot of mutual appreciation and warm applause, and when the young guitarist sang, it made me feel for all the world as if I were on a camping trip, with magic coming from mountains, balsams, and the clear perfumed air.

With this singer, there was also a sharing of other values. He sang about war, police, capitalism, poverty, and race discrimination. He was by turns serious and satiric, and his humor was shared by the crowd. He was about twenty, with long straight hair and a childlike expression, and with all that innocence I wondered how he could have learned so much, acquired so much sophistication about politics and economics. He seemed aware of things that the country's leaders were not aware of. There was a lot of rapport—people asked him for songs, and applauded his own choices as soon as he started them. He stopped, tuned, strummed and talked in a low voice to whomever was sitting by him. The whole crowd moved to the music, felt it and felt a sense of community with each other, and whether the people just walked by or stood for ten minutes, or really got into it and stayed for as long as the music continued, we all shared the whole scene. The music was a bond between us, a communication between us.

For me the most beautiful time for these impromptu concerts was after dinner when the twilight was coming on and Sproul Plaza had that same stillness that comes on a summer day when the wind dies down over a lake or in the woods. I felt the closeness of the Bay and the ocean—the hills deepened in hue, the sky over Marin took on colors, the air smelled of the sea, and then the guitar sang of all the terrible threats to that beauty: we felt the crassness and plasticness and brutality and exploitativeness of America, the America that ripped up and destroyed its trees and dumped poisons into the sea and imprisoned us in sooty, concrete ugliness; we felt that it was not necessary to be in jail to be imprisoned—Boston and New York can be prisons too; it was not necessary to be assaulted to experience violence—the bulldozer pushing earth around, brutally disturbing that fragile complex structure of roots and earthworms and burrows and organic fertile earth, was violence. We felt the intensity of the beauty and the horror of the threat, we felt the singer and the crowd, we felt music which was so sensual, so personal, so physical, so immediate that it was able to penetrate into us, able to unite us with other people and with the surroundings of nature, all of it saying, in Joni Mitchell's words, "We are stardust, we are golden, and we've got to get ourselves back to the garden." And the music, as the horizon over the Marin hills reddened and the fog rolled in through the Golden Gate and flecks of fog formed over the Berkeley hills, and the scene soft and tender and tingling at the edge of life—the music joined us together. In that moment, the music made us feel our oneness, our essential humanity, and our humanity as an aspect of nature, and we looked into each other, and the bright notes passed between us, flashing colors in the quiet dusk.

In the afternoons I usually left the campus and returned to my apartment to take a nap or to read. But if I felt restless, there was always more to see. And it was effortless, for the newness of Berkeley seemed inexhaustible.

Time and again there would be a stale period, when I would feel ennui creeping over me, when I would try to force myself to find something new and interesting and would of course fail, and then, just when it seemed impossible, the breeze would begin blowing. I would start out on a walk on the plain old streets of my residential neighborhood.

Wherever I went on the streets, interesting things were happening: a garage sale, a vegetable sale, a small truck being packed for a trip, an impromptu game or concert, dances, ball games, people lying in the grass reading, always the smiles that expressed the pleasures of the scene. Sometimes I would come across a tiny store or restaurant or coffeehouse that I had not noticed before or had sprung up overnight. Sometimes there would be a touch football or soccer game or a modern dance on the grassy part of some playground. Leather belts or candles for sale from somebody passing by. Three long-haired kids painting a small van. A boy sitting on the jutting second-story eave of a house, playing a guitar. Another person sitting cross-legged under a majestic tree. An old lady who smiled at the kids doing the painting, and who got smiles back. An exotic-looking woman reading on a doorstep. Little kids getting cold drinks. Just a boy or girl with a funny hat. Never before had I been in a place that was capable of this miracle, that seemed to be able to renew itself, that never yielded to déjà vu, that could not be written off, no matter how many times I walked the same street. I think this was possible for one reason beyond any other: so many people were putting so much imagination, creativity, and love into the making of life.

One prime example was the hitchhikers. I used to sit on a bench where I could watch them. Telegraph and Ashby was one good place, Telegraph and Dwight was another. Almost all wore marvelous freaky clothes, hats, beads, and colors. There was a great spirit of camaraderie among them. Some had signs. Many had knapsacks and sleeping bags. Some sat passively, hunched over. Some played instruments to pass the time. Some hustled the cars, getting out into the streets. They were great actors. Some implored, some appealed, some put on a whole comic act, some gestured in mock despair. Some got a ride immediately, others had a long wait. Once in a while there was a complete turnover of people; a hippie truck or bus came along and everyone, regardless of destination, just piled in and left. The hitchhikers seemed to be expressing this fantasy: on every major street in Berkeley, there was a moving belt of comfortable seats traveling in any direction one might wish to go. The hitchhikers did not waste money on a car, or unnecessary money for gas. They were not ruining the air or ecology. Not exhausting the earth, but banding together to preserve it. To the kids, driving in an automobile had been reborn as an adventure. Hitchhiking could be more fun than taking your own car. Think of the people you could meet, the lives you might hear about, the friends you may make, the unexpected events that lay ahead.

More than any place I had ever seen, Berkeley was

populated by people who seemed to be doing what they chose to do, rather than what they had to do. In Washington or at Yale, most people would tell me that they'd like to do X, but they had to do Y. They pictured themselves as slaves of duty. "I wish I could talk, but I have to finish this paper," a Yale student would say. Much Berkeley activity was not productive in the immediate sense, but contemplative. Often they were searching, rather than finding. Their "work" had become the serious business of gaining new awareness, new perspective on their lives.

In Berkeley, the people sitting in the sun were not on vacation. They were lying on the grass during working hours. They were there in prime time. They were not resting up from work. Those people lying there, in the summer of '67, had not stopped working, and they were not going to start again in a few minutes.

Berkeley culture was a proclamation of the freedom to choose. Before, people had always fitted their actions and their lives into decisions made by others, but now people would make new choices. And between the lives that were forced and programmed, and the new lives that could be more freely chosen, there was a great pause, a stopping, a vast sigh, after all that pressure—a chorus that went *aaaah, ooooooooh.* . . .

Occasionally I thought that the hippies represented some sort of closed society, some sort of in-group that demanded conformity as the price of being admitted. But gradually I came to feel that they were saying something quite different. They were doing something they wanted to do themselves, and they were inviting others to try it. Not demanding, just pointing—pointing to the activity, telling me to watch if I wanted to watch. They said: You're welcome to do it too if you want to. And you can do it entirely in your own way—you can invent a new way. And we'll help you if you want help. Watch us or not, join us or not, try it or not, whatever you do, it's okay.

The revolution that was happening in Berkeley was this: the kids, those beautiful kids, had discovered they could free their minds. They had not solved many problems yet, their own or anybody else's. The particular choices would have to come later. From here on it would be an inward adventure to find one's self and one's work. Out of many such discoveries the new forms would be found. We had received an intimation of how many of the limitations of life are really imaginary—are really walls which can be broken through.

I fully experienced it first on my late afternoon walk along College Avenue, with its views toward the western horizon, a walk that often coincided with the sunset. The sun went down across the Bay, beyond the Golden Gate, over the Marin hills, into the invisible Pacific. On nights when the fog was late in coming, the scattered clouds and the western sky lit up with a red and gold that was more brilliant than anything I had ever seen. There were glimpses of it all along College Avenue. But the sight that really caught me was not the sunset, but kids watching the sunset—the way they watched the sunset.

On the rooftops and balconies, hanging out of windows and on fire escapes and outside stairways, the silent figures faced the Bay, alone or in small groups, and watched, and there was a stillness everywhere. Their profiles showed the blue jeans, the long hair, the figures of youth. Sometimes the strains of rock music floated out on the air and blended with the mood. But it was the sense of wonder that was so special. On the rarest moments, when camping at some uniquely beautiful place—maybe by a wilderness lake or river, or better yet, high on a mountain, after a long day's hiking, with a mountain meal cooked—on those moments so rare I can remember them exactly ten or twenty or even thirty years later, I have felt such a perfect sense of wonder. Now it had come down to the streets.

I took to watching from my own bedroom window, and felt the same sense of quiet and wonder in myself. Some unseen people listened to rock music in a building near mine. Instead of being annoyed by it, I started to look forward to it, as if it were part of the sunset. I had never heard music like that before. The high, incredible notes that seemed to come from instruments that could imitate and surpass the human voice—what could be making those sounds? I couldn't believe it was electric guitars. The music seemed to be celebrating the discovery of unimagined new beauty and wonder. Mike had introduced me to some people who lived in that building, and one evening I ventured over to ask them what record was being played. They invited me to come up on the roof. The building was higher than those around us and had an uninterrupted view of San Francisco, with the lights just going on, and the bridges, and the traffic moving across them, and Berkeley and Oakland, and the dark Berkeley hills with lights just going on there too; we sat in all this wonder and beauty, still lit from the sunset, the Bay and the Marin hills and Mount Tamalpais, and in the foreground on the roof some silent kids, and the quiet and the wonder flowed to me as I just sat there, and when I was filled I went back to my apartment and cooked dinner.

How did I respond to everything I saw in Berkeley?

At first I totally disapproved and totally resisted. I could not enter into the spirit of things, or even accept what I saw as something good. I stayed absorbed in the self-imposed misery of a bad back, an island of resistance to everything, ready to return to New Haven after a week or two of this nonsense, the dignified Eastern visitor politely turning aside the excessive hospitality and enthusiasm of the natives.

I made no promises to Mike about how long I would stay in the apartment—perhaps only a week. My apartment in New Haven was ready and waiting if I wanted to go back to work; the house in the Adirondacks was there if I wanted the woods. If I chose to, I could think of this pause not as stopping, but as a couple of weeks in between activities, a well-deserved fortnight in a busy and productive year, a necessary convalescence before still greater exertions.

This stiffness in me was central to my initial state of mind. It was the Great Negator in full control, the person who automatically says no. How many times in my life after I have delivered my flat no, people have driven off to the beach for a picnic, and as soon as they have vanished I want desperately to join them. In Berkeley there was a new world and I had just fled from a sense of total frustration at Yale, yet I could not escape from being the disapproving Yale professor.

The first stage of coming to terms with my surroundings was the feeling that I was in Berkeley for a while, so I might as well make the best of things. By this I meant that I should start foraging for the necessities of life in this possibly uncivilized place, just as I would look around for dry wood to make a comforting campfire in the forest. It was necessary to find a laundry, a grocery store, a drugstore.

It was necessary to get toothpaste, razor blades, a place to buy the airmail edition of *The New York Times*. It was necessary to find a dry cleaner, and this was a tricky and difficult thing if one doesn't trust all dry cleaners equally. I had to stalk them, inspect them, make a choice. When I had located these things, I felt a sense of security, a sense of my own resourcefulness.

I was stiff, but there was another side of me that could yield. Especially I could yield to physical necessity like being ill and needing to rest. I could yield if everyone agreed there was no choice, if nobody (especially myself) could accuse me of neglecting what I should be doing. Slowly and subtly, my bad back gave me permission to yield a bit—all in the interest of a faster recovery. Doctor's orders, so to speak. That hearty, mythical doctor said, "I *insist* that you take care of yourself for a change; I *order* you to take a vacation; I want you to promise me you'll slow down." Relaxation was acceptable because it was doing me some good, restoring me to health. Relaxation, for once, was necessary.

The power that I possessed to yield, once I accepted the idea, was surprisingly great. I have always been able to find a deep pleasure in submitting to a force more powerful than myself. If the Great Negator's fear and pride and concern about what others will think are calmed, I can yield cheerfully, accepting the confines of a hospital room or a temporary enforced stay in a town where my automobile has broken down, and be creative about the place where I find myself. It feels good when the warrior can rest.

What Berkeley and my bad back demanded and permitted was that I stop. I must neither work nor climb mountains. I must settle for idleness and a few short walks in the neighborhood. I could let the engine inside myself be idle, the engine that was not meant to rest even a moment until at last it broke down.

Gradually, day by day I could feel a small relaxing, an imperceptible slowing down of something inside myself. After coming back from an early-morning walk on College Avenue when the sun came out brightly from the overnight fog, I would go downstairs and stand in front of my house, just taking in the sun's warmth. I think this started with looking for the mail, which came at ten or ten-thirty, and soon I began to wait for the postman to arrive as a regular part of the day. Across the street were several houses with extraordinarily beautiful flowers on their front lawns and vines trailing up to their second floors. I would cross over to look at them.

The changes that came were subtle. I noticed how many people walked around with bare feet, and one day I tried coming downstairs with bare feet and even ventured across the street that way, and it felt exciting and new—the warm pavement and wet grass underneath. I also saw that many people went around with their shirts off, and one day I tried that for a few minutes, too. I felt self-conscious and embarrassed. A dignified person like me, a person with a serious job, looking absurd in bare feet and a bare, naked torso on a city street. Imagine if I had walked into the law school that way! But I felt secure in the idea that no one who knew me was likely to come walking down Derby at mid-morning, and so, with a feeling of sneaky shame, I did it when the sun was warm. After all, I was convalescing, wasn't I? Like a character in Thomas Mann's *The Magic Mountain,* I felt the sun was thawing out a stiffness in my soul, a stiffness that went back so many years.

I grew less self-conscious. At Yale, everything and everybody conspired to make me feel that way. When I was in law school, I was so frightened of being called on by the teacher in class that I would hide in the back or not even come to class or say "unprepared" rather than answer. If I did answer, I feared I would totally forget the facts of the case I was talking about and be unable to complete a coherent sentence. I felt I would shake myself to fragments right there in front of everybody. And that was true even when I was editor-in-chief of the *Yale Law Journal,* the ranking potentate of that status-conscious world!

Here I could take off my shoes or my shirt, I could sit down on the pavement, I could stand in the middle of the plaza and stare, I could lie down in the grass, I could find an unoccupied bench, somewhere farther away where benches weren't in such demand, and stretch out full-length on it. I could laugh or do a little dance. And whatever I did, no one would make me feel self-conscious. I was cutting back the layers of complication in my life, cutting back the things that made me hurry and worry, and the result of that cutting back was a rich, sensual, sunny simplicity.

Necessities, goals, plans, complexities were falling off, like unnecessary wrappings. Something softer, slower, simpler was emerging. In the new simplicity, there was pleasure in going down to the Derby Food Mart (marked with a picture of a derby hat) for a few groceries. Pleasure—a truly sensual pleasure—in washing out a nylon shirt and hanging it up to dry. Pleasure in the simplest and most ordinary activity. When I was really feeling serene and slow, I discovered to my amazement that the mail, instead of being much-anticipated, became a bother. It was likely to contain frowns and worries and complexities from back

East, things to intrude on the sun and flowers, an unwelcome interruption that, if it was bad enough, might spoil irretrievably the mood of the morning.

Out of my enforced idleness I began to make a discovery. I learned that if I slowed down, things in my immediate surroundings became more interesting, more capable of giving me good feelings. A shrub outside my bedroom window that meant nothing to me when I was in a hurry could give pleasure if I lay back and yielded to it. Just watching the sun's reflections move slowly across the wall could give me pleasure.

Mike's apartment was more sensual and tactile, more full of sights and feelings than my apartment in New Haven. My own apartment had a stiff living room "for guests," a bedroom, and kitchen. I had no television, and a record player that was not suited to stereo dated from when I was a high school freshman in 1943. There was nothing meaningful to look at, inside or outside. It was just a base, a place to keep one functioning. Mike's apartment had pillows, a stereo set, posters, plants, color, light, an invitation to do nothing but enjoy what was there. I found the invitation tempting.

That apartment—I was starting to give myself to it, let it enrich me, and give me a sense of calm. I was starting to cherish it. It was as if I were somebody other than the Eastern me, a new body and a new mind, and that sunny green apartment was a new place and a new life and, if I let my imagination just wander, that somebody could be me, that person—bare feet and shorts in the living room, surrounded by all those bright posters and plants and pillows and the trees and shrubs outside—that person—I could imagine just for a moment of delicious freedom—that person—I could feel the wish and the dream and the long-

denied stirring and the adventure and the stiff closing off—
that person could be me.

I was concentrating on a few blocks, a few sights—
enriching my feelings each day. Everything outside this
focus detracted. I learned that even pleasures diminished
the focus and thereby reduced, rather than added to, my
happiness—like a ride to San Francisco with Mike to eat at
the Tadich Grill, or a Sunday drive to Marin, or a pleasant
visit to some Berkeley friends of my own age. Even a walk
beyond the precincts—a walk, let us say, to Oakland or up
toward the Claremont Hotel or toward the beautiful homes
on the North campus side—took me away from my center.
To show how this worked: after one of these excursions
(perhaps a walk up Euclid on the Northside), I came back
not refreshed, but more impatient with my own surroundings.

How little it took—one frustrating, disturbing call, one
wrong visitor—to destroy the fragile openness that I was
discovering in Berkeley. What staggered my mind was that
in the New Haven or Washington worlds these interruptions came along at an overwhelming rate, and they were
devastatingly more powerful. They had a cumulative,
numbing effect. No wonder the magic I had been feeling
in Berkeley had eluded me for so long. One trip in New
Haven to Brown and Thomas Automobile Service, with a
wait for the service manager and then arriving at Yale on
foot after an unpleasant, ugly walk through automobile row
on Whalley Avenue—that would be enough to destroy the
fragile feeling in me for a day. The miracle which brought
me out to Berkeley had given the magic a chance. I became
aware of this, and began to fight the interference in order
to allow the changes to happen.

A crucial fact about Berkeley was the absence of people whose presence would trigger my old roles. The whole Berkeley experience was made possible by not having to be in my role. Instead of performing for people or responding to expectations, I started to share. I shared experiences with people I didn't know, without ever exchanging a word. For once I could just look and see what other people were doing. I was ready to become a watcher.

Something in me began to respond to what I was seeing, by letting my imagination add to what was there. I increasingly made the sights and events of the day into something special. The simplest routine, such as breakfast at the terrace cafeteria on the campus, with *The San Francisco Chronicle* and a conversation I could listen to at the next table—could give me pleasure.

I was also depressed in Berkeley a good deal of the time. I was very lonely; there was not a single person, not even Mike, who I saw regularly or felt close to in any way. I had nothing to do either in my apartment or outside; my whole day was a fragile effort to feel good, and often my spirits sagged and I thought about my unused plane ticket to the East. Nights could be particularly lonely and depressing. My bad back made me feel old and unwell. Frequently I totally disbelieved in what I was seeing around me. Instead of a transformation, I saw bizarre fads, mindless spasms, people plugged in to electronic impulses. I felt sated with their aggressive silliness, wishing I were back at serious work. It was these many periods of bad feeling that gave Berkeley a chance to demonstrate its power of renewal.

Bare feet, casual clothes, lazy mornings were small symbols of the new way that I began to feel. I was more at ease, more free, more flowing, more funny, less intense. I learned to take it easy. I felt that good things would effort-lessly come my way. I felt that more would come from sitting still than from trying to make things happen. I felt softer and more gentle. It was not so essential that I try to understand everything, or worry over everything. I was more spontaneous. I had a greater confidence that life would treat me fairly, even if I didn't keep sternly watching it every moment. At times I felt like a happy child.

Much of what I saw and heard reached secret places in me. The bright sunny streets with flowers made me feel like a child in a secret garden. The notes of electric guitars re-opened my mind to floating images and colors I used to see as a child when I closed my eyes, something I never thought I could share with anyone.

From being a watcher I became an adherent to what I felt was a cause. If it stood for many of the things I believed in politically, giving me allies that I had never expected to find, if it made me feel good, relaxed, and happy, if it reached out to me when I was in a lonely and depressed place in my life, and if it could evoke the secret places in me and show me that others felt and believed as I did—then in every way it was *my* cause. Was it possible that anyone but me, in fact, a large group of people seemingly quite different from me, wanted what I wanted? If so, I was not alone any more in the way I had always believed myself to be alone, for my yearnings were not unique and need not be secret. I could accept these people as being like myself. I could abandon thinking myself special and privileged, and although I was a highly educated, high-status eastern intel-lectual and a professor at Yale, I could accept them as my equals, my own species. Then and only then could my aloneness be ended.

I was deeply moved and grateful. I was ready to believe in this cause: encourage it, expand it, and give myself to it. I was ready to join it and fight for it. I saw it as a fight for myself.

In keeping with the general atmosphere, I was resolved to do no "work." A flow of new scenes and impressions proceeded through me and began to emerge in the form of thoughts, ideas, reflections. My mind came alive. A month earlier in New Haven I had felt mentally stale. Left alone at Yale, my mind tended to go blank with boredom in attempts to rearrange old thoughts.

Something began to happen to me on my College Avenue walks. At first it seemed to be by courtesy of Mr. J. K. Galbraith. His book *The New Industrial State* caught my interest and excitement. I never felt free to mark up books even if I owned them. But now I began underlining and then started writing notes and ideas in the margin. This impromptu notebook began a new epoch in my life. It led me to buy my first green notebook. One day I was at the U.C. Bookstore and saw a pile of medium-sized 35-cent spiral notebooks with green-lined paper; I bought one—the first of many it turned out, and of many other sorts of notebooks as varied as types of days, that came later—and found that without any effort at all I was writing things down in it.

The pale green paper of the notebooks was important to me because green had become identified with the corduroy jeans kids wore in Berkeley. Green was the color of a notebook's pages, which, like the miraculous pitcher of milk in mythology, filled up by themselves. I had written law review articles, legal briefs, and some magazine articles and had prepared classes and made speeches, but only by purposeful effort. A notebook that filled up by itself—that was something entirely new.

If I carefully left the notebooks and their accompanying pencils at home and set out for just a walk, within a few blocks my mind would start to flow with ideas and I would have to stop at a drugstore and buy whatever sort of notebook or pad, and pencil or pen was available, and hurry to a bench and start writing things down. Then I would have a new and odd-shaped notebook or pad, or in extreme cases even a few paper napkins, to add to my collection.

What began to fill up those pages was notes on Galbraith, mixed in with stuff like phone numbers and lists saying "buy toothpaste, get laundry"—and then, slowly and imperceptibly, notes on ideas, theories and impressions. I would be on College Avenue and an idea would come from within. Forced to sit down on one of those benches meant for bus passengers, I opened my notebook, and let my pencil start writing.

If I walked along the streets, I felt what it might be like to be an artist. I could sit and take nourishment from my own thoughts. I could walk along and look at almost anything and draw some meaning or pleasure from it. On my canvas I could include freeways, hitchhikers, television crime shows, corrupt public officials, and the new consciousness culture I saw all around me. I could spend days drifting in and out of bookstores, watching check-out lines at the supermarket, sniffing around stores that sold incense, waiting in line at the bank, sitting in the lobby of a hotel watching people—and all of that time I would be learning, creating, working.

This feeling of being an artist gave me great calm. I saw many of the young people in Berkeley as fellow artists, and felt I was part of a community. I felt a fullness to my days.

A Sunday—just lying in bed awake, looking at the world outside—the cloudy, cool morning, the foliage, the slowly moving light—listening to the birds, just lying there thinking and feeling good. Yes, a sense of well-being, of no hurry to go anywhere, of the high fog clouds like a cool warm blanket that gave permission to stay in bed, no urgent demand to rush out and do something, the high stratus fog saying lie there, the day isn't up yet, the sun isn't ready yet. And then I said to myself: just lie there feeling good, let the thoughts flow to you, flow in from the ocean, from the Bay, or from the west wind, let the free open good new thoughts be gently blown in the partly open window, rattling the glass just enough, feel free and easy, no rush, no obligations, no effort needed, nothing demanded, nothing to do, no one to visit, nowhere to go, just let the natural gentle forces flow, let the influences prevail, let the breeze—or rather the so slowly moving air—let it come and touch you.

I could lie there and float. I could lie there and be lifted. I could lie there and be touched and cared for. Life, energy, warmth—they could flow into me. I could open a porthole, a valve, a lock inside myself, and life could flow in—impressions, feeling, hopes. I could go exploring by lying still. I could lie still and go places on a magic carpet. To go to some new place, I did not have to work up inner energy—get in a car, and struggle to drive to a beach or a mountain. Those magic places, the bare rocks, the pinnacles with sunset light on them, the remote quiet ponds and mysterious forest, the blue blue distant mountain ranges— they were not only to be reached by driving, driving with high-test gasoline, tense nerves, and the power of my will —no, I could be taken there. I could be open, so that life would act upon me. I could be able to listen, to feel, to see —to stop talking, forcing, controlling, worrying, making impressions, being approved of. To stop being an intellectual who judges and criticizes and appraises and compares but cannot be moved or changed or touched, who cannot see or feel or hear or know.

And when I lay still, just lying there and breathing and feeling, when I lay there like that, the flow of my life was reversed. And I who had gone all of my life on my own inner energy, burning up some inner fuel, parts working and wearing out, driving, driving, driving, work, classes, tests, teaching, visits, efforts and still greater efforts, horse-power and candlepower, staying lit by determination alone. I who strained and struggled, who bit fingernails down to the quick, who chewed paper and rubber bands and handkerchiefs and towels until my teeth chipped, I who sweated until my shirts were drenched and smelly, who shook and trembled, who strained and forced, who lived each moment by a titanic effort of the will, I could lie back and life would come to me. . . .

For this was my Turning. Let something happen to me, let something softly caress me. Be soft, be quiet, be open, be helpless, be still. I am soft, small, open, vulnerable, gentle. I want to be held and stroked and petted and ruffled and cuddled and tickled and cooled and warmed and held tightly. The quiet clouds, the moving air—they are strong, they are big, they have gentleness and power, they will lay soft and strong and firm and warm and gentle on my warm, quiet body. And I don't have to do anything, go anywhere, wind myself up to effort, perform, carry out duties, exercise initiative, fulfill expectations or responsibilities. There is something in the world larger than me. Something that will take care of things even if I don't. I who thought the world would stay there only if I held it with my own effort, I now can lie in the cradle of something that can, that will, hold me. Let the cool come, and the damp, and the warmth, let the time pass, let the sunlight move, let the leaves rustle. Touch me and rock me.

When I returned to Yale from Berkeley in the fall of 1967, nothing had visibly changed. Yale students were what they had always been—nice, clean, polite, respectful, narrowly focused on college activities and careers. They often followed a routine: classes in the morning, athletics in the afternoon, study at night, with perhaps a few beers at a club or fraternity, and football weekends with dates from a women's college. They were also intelligent, ironical, and not too spoiled by the world. I waited to see what would happen.

At Yale I had been a law teacher for eight years, and a college teacher for one year. From the beginning, I loved Yale and I loved being a professor. At a single step I had gone from being a hard-pressed legal employee in a profession I never came to terms with, to being a lord in a Gothic kingdom. Yale was solid, established, aristocratic, secure. I had all the privileges and facilities of a great institution, and a position that carried substantial respect in the outside world. I could teach whatever I wanted, and design my life in any way that I wanted. The faculty supported the most extreme degree of sovereign independence for each member. There were libraries, museums, a theater, a magnificent gymnasium. There were receptions, cocktail parties, greetings wherever I went. Good morning, Professor, the barber or the druggist would say.

An endless flow of young people filled with questions,

ideas, fresh enthusiasm, was the most rewarding and life-giving part of my job. The first day of class I would survey the new faces and feel excited about all the possibilities they represented. I would learn where they came from, what interests they had had in high school and college, and see them as friends and an ever-present source of renewal.

I threw all my energy into my teaching, and felt a deep satisfaction and contentment. Fall Days, Snowy Days, Dark Wet Days, the steamy showers at the Gym, drinks at Mory's, looking for new books at the bookstore, sitting behind my desk talking to students, Class at Eleven, Class at Two—all high points in a life that I loved and hoped would never end.

But as my colleagues moved to large houses on tree-lined St. Ronan Street or to country homes in the surrounding area, entertaining elegantly and sending their children to private schools, I remained in a small apartment I had taken when I first arrived in New Haven, situated in a group of tacky, cheaply constructed apartment houses built mainly for young couples with children in the diaper stage, listening to babies cry through the paper-thin walls, and spraying for the ants and roaches that invaded the newly built kitchen.

Yale was a habitat perfectly suited to fastidious, fussy eccentrics whose concern with one or another scholarly specialty led them to lose the ability to carry on the more ordinary functions of life. Before I could settle down to work or get to sleep at night, everything had to be just so. I needed and depended on the right pillow, the right laundry for my shirts, the right butcher, the right doctors for various ailments. I was always careful of my bad back. I was stiff, anxious, full of small rituals, very precise about time.

The dignity of my position prevented me from being playful and made me embarrassed when carrying my own laundry.

There was plenty of social life, but all of a very formal kind—cocktail parties where students gathered in small circles around the professors, faculty dinner parties full of polite small talk, an occasional dinner with a group of law students who questioned me respectfully. Mostly I stayed at home, returning to the library for late evening work.

Gradually I accepted as my personal fate that I would always be alone. I would never be married. I would never have a family. I would never have any one person to whom I was most important and who was most important to me. To accept this was to give something up, something I had cherished nearly all my life. Perhaps in my deepest soul I did not give it up. But my practical day-to-day self gave it up. And so I commenced to construct the best possible life for one person alone.

I was extremely self-conscious about being so alone, and found places to shop or walk where I thought no one would see me. I would cringe if I met a married law student in the supermarket, my shopping cart too obviously filled with items for one person, my dinner of frozen peas and ground beef displayed for anyone to see. To be alone was always to have one's face marked by pain and sadness, however much one smiled and laughed. Each friendship was accepted with a resigned sense that it could meet no real needs and therefore was only slightly better than being alone.

From my earliest days of teaching at the law school, I wanted to be an educator in the best sense of the word. There were thousands of young people spending three to ten years in a university community, with playing fields, dining halls, communal residences, scholars—a shelter from some of the pressures of the outside world. I hoped that this situation would give me opportunity to encourage creativity, imagination, enthusiasm. I wanted to help young people to realize their potential. I thought students should learn from each other, and I from them.

To make any of this possible, I came to realize that I had to start by helping students to believe in themselves. Unless they felt that they were deserving, were worthy, were intelligent and gifted, and that their ideas were genuinely wanted by others, their minds would remain blocked. I felt that my job was to reach and stimulate the minds of my students. To do this, I needed to relate to them in a very different way than did a remote lecturer. There should be personal closeness, real feeling, real caring, trust. And the teacher should be open to learning from the student, for unless there was equality, unless the student also had power to teach, there could only be a one-way process, no genuine flow.

Since each student was a unique individual, there could be no single standard of value, and hence the pressure of competition and grades should not be paramount. Every student's ideas were different, so every student should receive respect. There should be time, continuity, space, ease.

But no matter how hard I tried to live within this system, I was increasingly forced to confront the fact that my job asked for the wrong things from me, and often prevented me from doing what I most believed in. Teaching was the most clearly defined job. Then there was the writing of scholarly articles—necessary for promotion, tenure, and professional standing, as well as the key to my continued intellectual aliveness. But being a faculty member also meant having to attend long and difficult faculty and committee meetings several times a week, sometimes involving many exhausting hours. Then there were my institutional obligations—public service, helping outside legal causes, talking to groups in the law school or the university, testifying at legislative hearings, dealing with student grievances. When was I to catch up on my reading, go for a swim, have time for friends, for thinking, for myself?

At first I tried to do everything. But slowly I realized the true situation: there was six or ten times more to do than any human being could do. And at the same time, much of what I had to do turned out, after a very large investment, to accomplish little. The endless round of faculty and committee meetings produced volumes of talk about relatively minor issues that never seemed to get resolved. In the public realm I could give myself to endless good causes without feeling that I was making a dent in society's problems. I could be busy every waking minute and still go almost insane with frustration.

Even when I could focus on teaching, too much was against my ideas. The school was dominated by intense competition and by a focus on grades, on professional jobs which depended on grades, on recommendations, and on a view of law as a game and a livelihood rather than as a search for values. The serious business of the students was sharpening their weapons and landing a job. It was against all odds when a truly educational spirit could be ignited in the classroom. I wanted to stop competition, stop being an authority, stop inequality, give up the professor's role. I wanted to reduce the importance of grades, substitute papers for examinations. I wanted to stop letting all my time be frittered away in nonproductive bureaucratic ways. My position was difficult: I was forced to look irresponsible in the eyes of other professors and the school administration, while trying to be truly responsible according to my own standards of what was important.

And so my strange position was that I must increasingly refuse to do the job that was expected of me in order to be able to do the work that was needed and that I believed in. I had to fight against institutional anarchy, and for my beliefs, almost always alone and without feeling able to explain myself.

It was against this background that I waited to see if the Berkeley spirit would come to Yale. For months, nothing at all happened. Within a year however, the campus had been transformed. It seemed as if a new university had replaced the old. The grim courtyards were festive with music and art. Many students wore colorful and individualistic clothes instead of the uniform collegiate apparel of a year earlier. Spontaneity replaced the campus routine for many students. Gothic Yale, set in drab, industrial New Haven, had become beautiful.

The changes came to one individual at a time, and they could be quite sudden and spectacular. It seemed as if less than a month, maybe only a week, perhaps just a day was required for a transformation to begin. One day a student was part of the system, resisting new ideas, intensely competitive and defending the Vietnam war. The next day he had gone from grey, wormlike, earthbound caterpillar to butterfly.

Such transformations were possible because they were not the sudden acceptance of some foreign and external teaching, but an awakening—the release of some life force already within. It was a blinding new awareness and permission. Numbness was pierced, and the long-slumbering child was invited to come out and be filled with love and wonder at the world.

One student and then another would be touched with magic. Some caught it from roommates, some from friends or teammates or even from hearing a concert. Marijuana and sometimes LSD were important catalysts for many. Whatever assistance these drugs gave could have come from some other means. The essential change was a new way of seeing and feeling, and drugs were a mere instrument to that end. Nevertheless, drugs were a primary instrument at that time. They opened the doors to new knowledge both within and without.

What was a student like who had gone through such growth? We all saw the external things—a crew cut transformed to long curly locks, khaki pants to bell-bottoms, neckties to beaded necklaces, frowns to smiles. But the growth itself was not on the surface. In each individual it was different, but still I came to see important similarities.

If I were allowed only one word, I would say they were responsible. Students took responsibility for being more aware of themselves, of others, of the universe; for pursuing knowledge of all kinds; for seeking and having a standard of social ethics; and for the consequences of their own actions to themselves, to other people who might be affected, to society and the planet. Gone from them were those qualities of Yale students which so often allowed them to be indifferent to learning, to other people's feelings, to the community—leaving a mess for others to clean up, hurting the feelings of a mismatched weekend date from one of the women's colleges, studied indifference to the books they were assigned to read. The new students were better citizens. They took more responsibility for their own education, their fellow students, their professors and parents, their university, their world, than any students I had known.

Of all the qualities that I saw, the most spiritual and beautiful was the freedom to be a happy child. To be a child like that was incredibly far from the protected, defended, stylized persona that Yale students usually showed. The happy child was secure, beautiful, trusting, unworried, open and interested in everything, a person who cries immediately when hurt. This was the child behind the pure, sweet faces that were the outward look of many new consciousness people. The outside world had trouble understanding that child, and usually assumed it to be something else, most often a grown-up but irresponsible person pretending to be small so as to get away with breaking the rules. Of course there were many hippie versions of the latter person. But there were also many true versions of the happy child. To me, so accustomed to people who held back emotion, that child was a welcome gift.

The faces are what I remember best. I could never get over how much beauty, strength, and spirituality shone in the faces.

The gateway to the new world was mind expansion. When students at Yale stepped through the barriers into a new awareness of their minds and senses it was like the moment in the film version of *The Wizard of Oz* when black and white changes to color. So many things could be seen as never before. So many things became beautiful. So many other things were seen in their true ugliness and harmfulness. Suddenly many people were thrilled with the fun and joy of vastly expanded perception and knowledge. Every person had an infinite mind, and could travel as far as he or she wished, and share where others had traveled.

When the students looked at cars pouring into Whalley Avenue, they could see and feel the metallic ugliness, poisonous fumes, and noise. When they looked at people, they could see fears, insecurities, trust or lack of trust, happiness, vulnerability, and façades. Students felt far more messages from their bodies. They caught the lurking shadows of the occult, the mystical, the unknown. They could listen to the rhythm and crunch and texture of an unseen person walking. They could see what a profound thing a foreign language might be, or the patterns formed by many birds. They could stare at the flame of a match and think of the discovery of fire.

The new students were more respectful and reverent and full of wonder than almost any adults I had ever known. If you showed them a print of a great painting—perhaps we were sitting on the floor in somebody's dormitory room at Yale—they looked at it with as much joy and amazement as an art expert might feel if an unknown and even greater Leonardo were suddenly discovered. It was as if they had never seen anything before—trees, plants, sculpture, paintings, the sun. And they discovered these wonders not as small children but as college students with the capacity to appreciate fully how marvelous it was to have a world full of wonders. People smiled at one another all the time. They were smiling because the world was so beautiful. They were smiling at all the unlimited wonders that were available to be shared. Their smiles said, "Isn't this warm sun wonderful?" "Don't you like the rain?" "Look at all those great people." "Isn't this line at the check-cashing window ridiculous?" "Isn't it fun to be on the other side?" The other side!

Mind expansion also led to seeing many established ways of thinking as dangerously irrational, such as the society's reliance on force or its indifference to the needs of the planet as a whole. The new consciousness people saw the destructiveness of America as perhaps no group had ever seen it before. They saw the dishonesty, the phoniness, the hypocrisy. They felt the cruelty, the lack of caring, the irresponsibility hiding under ignorance. They clearly saw a national bias against intelligence, sensitivity, awareness. They did not react with cynicism, but with commitment. *We* are the people, we expect more of ourselves, they said. It is our country and we love it, and we have a right to be angry, to be disgusted, to be outraged, and to expect greatness. We have believed the high ideals of America; we will not accept a betrayal of those ideals, such as the Vietnam war.

The students saw that society had plans for them—business, the professions, or worse yet, the draft and the war, which would mean the end of freedom and the beginning of alienation and damage and imprisonment in a sterile environment. They saw how empty and unfulfilling middle-class life could become. They recognized that the goals of money, ambition and power were a trap. When they said "Hell no, we won't go," they meant not only the war but also the whole corporate structure and the accompanying materialistic way of life. They wanted to make an alternative future for themselves.

There was little cynicism and there was—there had to be—much laughter. It was all so absurd. The empty political speeches. The way public officials took themselves seriously. The unconvincing television commercials. The stereotyped, unreal social forms, such as men loudly greeting each other at a company banquet. An American President pretending folksiness while surrounded by armed guards and bulletproof automobiles. Gigantic Cadillacs using up gasoline. When all of it was seen at once, and for the first time, the "serious" world was totally exposed. The students could spend hours, days, weeks just laughing, just crying.

Mind expansion led directly to a remarkable increase of creative energy. Music was one great interest, and it was unbelievable to me how many students discovered their own musical talent and played with so much feeling and imagination. People had the energy to seek out and get to know many people outside their normal group of friends. They were always trying new things: acting in a play, inventing a ceremony or ritual, doing a photo montage on a wall, painting the hall with fluorescent paint, making a snowman, teaching ghetto kids at a nearby school, writing letters to the editor. You could move around the Yale campus all day and never come to an end of the richness of things to see and do and people to talk to. There were gatherings, outdoor music, costumes, skits, posters and paintings, poetry readings.

In all that was said and written about the late 1960's, there was little praise for energy as such. Vast amounts of criticism were leveled at certain uses of energy—for example, campus demonstrations that got out of hand—but no one seemed to observe that the real miracle was the energy itself.

There were so many examples of releases of energy. "We can change the world" was a line in one of the important songs of the times, and people felt this and believed it.

From outside the new consciousness, concern was focused almost exclusively on that culture's supposed excesses of passion and enthusiasm, but the main fact was that people *did* care, that they *did* want to do something, that they *did* believe that their actions would have some effect.

The same energy was displayed in the marvelous sensuality and freedom of the period. From observing, I learned the fact that sensuality is a form of energy and not a form of lazy indulgence. In truth, sensuality takes great energy. Go to the beach when you have very little energy, and you will not be able to do much with all the beauty and freedom that is available. But take a walk when you have high energy, and there will be so much to look at that you will forget yourself completely: you will see children's games, you will see interaction between people, you will observe humanity with the eye of an artist. You can enter into the scene by smiling at anyone and receiving energy back.

Freedom and spontaneity also take high energy. Many times during the late 1960's the thought occurred to me that freedom is profoundly misunderstood in America. We are taught to believe that freedom consists of having the right to be free, but freedom really consists of actually being free. You do the unexpected, you change your routine, you sweep yourself and other people into adventure, you act on impulse, you move fast, you change your pace quickly, and you are open to whatever event follows.

In terms of human potential, perhaps the most telling fact about the release of energy in the late 1960's was that it led to an incredible amount of inventiveness and creativity in people. The culture was so rich that within the space of a few years it produced comic book art, psychedelic posters, elaborate experiments with lighting, profound changes in dress and ornamentation, experiments with astrology and religion, and a whole new era in music. It produced a new use of the streets, the parks, and other public places; it produced new gestures and handshakes; it allowed new experiments with personal appearance, from beards and beads to body paint. It opened up new fields of knowledge, such as natural foods and body awareness. An underground press grew up.

I was familiar with a legal system that regarded human energy as a danger to be controlled and repressed. Now I clearly saw that human energy is something sacred and divine.

Energy was dependent on good feelings. Therefore the students were concerned with actually experiencing good feelings, not with intellectually knowing they are possible. The students saw that society did not consider actual feelings to be important. It was indifferent to how good or bad people felt. It put all sorts of obstacles in the way of the ability to feel at all. Now the rebellion began. The students believed that how happy we feel, how much love we are able to feel, are important and should never be ignored by society for the sake of any other goal.

The concern with feelings produced unlooked-for discoveries involving perception, awareness, sensitivity, aesthetics, sensuality, love and community. The alienation imposed by society turned out to be a wall of ignorance about many things that profoundly concerned the human species.

The most important word was love. The students were willing to let their feelings and enthusiasm flow freely in many directions. They could love the morning, love seeing their friends, love what they ate for breakfast, love the outrageous maroon bell-bottoms they wore, love the objects in their rooms. It was discovered that love was not in limited supply. Out of an abundance of love came a sense of community. I knew of no other group of people who showed such generosity toward individuals who came their way. It was respect and it was understanding, not "tolerance." It was acceptance of each person's humanity, nothing less. This extended to an unusual sensitivity toward older people. The students seemed to have a natural grace in relating to everyone. Walking through the cafeteria line, they brought smiles to the faces of the people who served the food.

There was a high degree of caring. Students cared about injustices, about civil liberties, about the way people were treated in prisons and mental hospitals. They cared about issues like old age, issues normally ignored by youth. This showed most brilliantly in the time they would take out of their own lives to work in the community or with mental patients or with some fellow student in the dormitory who was upset and in need of help. These were people who could unselfconsciously ask everyone to silently join hands before a meal at someone's home.

In the media, violence and self-destruction were ascribed to the young people of the late sixties. I saw just the opposite: I saw the gentlest, sweetest, least violent people I had ever known. The spirit that I knew was opposed to violence, and consistently sought calm and inner peace.

One day some students were playing football on the grass behind Ezra Stiles College, and I sat down on a low wall to watch. The players had their hair tied in headbands. They didn't just play the game, they frolicked. They showed affection for one another. They let their imaginations work. The players were really *playing.* What a misused word! When they caught a long pass, they leaped up in the air in playful self-congratulation. This touch football game gave way to moments of joy, to mock showing-off, to moments of affection (when two people, a play just completed, would come up and hug each other and then continue the game). And then there were the pile-ups. Two people fell down, and more people piled on, not for any reason, just to pile on.

All at once, without any signal or agreement they started playing tackle football in slow motion, like a television replay of a pro football game. They formed two lines facing each other, centered the ball, someone received it and ran; finally he was tackled and went down in slow motion, rolling over in the grass until a couple of people piled on top of him. And this tableau continued, this "game," this ballet, this dance, this expression of happiness kept on until it was over, just naturally over, and everyone went his way.

It was a self-conscious revolution. The students talked about it all the time. It was never a movement that needed or wanted leaders. Every person could be great and a genius in some way—that was its rebellion and its vision.

The change in the students gave me my chance. Bit by bit I found myself contriving a scheme to become an entirely new kind of teacher and thereby vastly improve my own life. I would teach a college course concerning contemporary American society, in which the problems of alienation would be discussed along with the ideas I had evolved in law school. Then the course would deal with the stage of new consciousness, and I would try to put it into perspective as a development seeking to reverse the process of alienation. Teaching would begin in the classroom, but it would not end there. It would continue wherever students wanted to learn—at lunch, at the gym, in students' rooms, outside the library, or in small groups that met in the evenings. There would be reading to offer further perspective, papers to write—but never an exam. Grades would be less relevant, minimizing competition. The papers could be as highly individual, creative and fun as the students were able to make them. "Use this as a chance to do something that you would enjoy, that will stretch your mind," I would say.

There were economic and sociological analyses, attempts at theory, short stories, autobiographical and family sketches, photographic essays, an occasional song with lyrics and music, a few collages and other pictorial works of art. My faith in the students was rewarded. They spent far more time on projects for my class than on the usual term paper. My work also became my pleasure and my education, and my apartment and office were festooned with interesting and beautiful things created by my students.

At the same time I began a major project of inviting the students to teach me directly about new consciousness. I recognized the force of new consciousness as something greater than any individual; therefore the students' knowledge, as initial receptors of the culture, was greater than mine. They were the sensitive antennas. The new messages would reach them first. I recognized my unique opportunity and became a learner from my own students. By 1969 there were literally hundreds of "teachers" available to me, and all of my learning could be done firsthand. To make this possible, I gave up my role as an authority figure, as someone who insisted on looking and acting and being treated differently from the students, and became as conscientious a student of theirs as I hoped they would be of me. I gave all of my time and energy to it, doing only enough work at the law school to keep things going. I started listening to college students early in the morning and continued until late at night, seven days a week, for two years. I did not merely listen, I tried everything myself. I was an anthropologist, but I was also a participant, an experimenter.

This was my elaborate research project for what became *The Greening of America*. Even when I was having the most fun, I was careful to observe and record what I was learning, and I always asked the students not only to share their fun, but, whether it was music or literature or a new attitude toward life, to share their knowledge.

On the days when I would teach my college course I got up early in the morning, full of excitement. Although I had prepared the main outline of my lecture the day before, I always left it unfinished, awaiting the morning's inspiration. The fact that I both insisted on and found inspiration, that I could confidently wait until the last minute for it, showed how much I had changed. I worked while having breakfast, and the pinging sound of the radiant heating pipes in my apartment sounded musical. I felt so good. Until I started this course in 1967 I had rarely lectured, just conducted law school give-and-take discussions. Now I was a full-scale performer, and loving it.

On the best mornings I walked, often through crunchy snow in the clear cold, feeling glad to be alone because the ideas were still flowing. I went to the dining hall at Ezra Stiles College, found a table by myself, got some coffee and unfolded *The New York Times,* which I read while still going over my lecture. The students at other tables smiled and said hello, but knew that I should be left undisturbed. They did come over if they had an important message, such as a concert they would like me to go to that afternoon, or just a pat on the back and "I'm really looking forward to class today, Charles."

Many students called me by my first name, which was seldom done with other professors at that time. I was a teacher who, the students thought, belonged to them. They gave me just the right air of friendly encouragement, expectation, family business for later on, and space while I worked. Then there were always one or more to accompany me when it was time to walk over to the classroom.

The lectures I gave became *The Greening of America,* and some of their flavor is recorded there. I used many kinds of illustrations, often reading from the morning newspapers, quoting from legal opinions, describing my years in Washington, D.C., reading from Dickens or Ruskin, telling about a conversation I had had the day before with students outside the library. I was usually full of energy, humor, passion. I could laugh with the class, and share feelings with them. Sometimes I would think of a new idea in midflight, in front of the whole class, and would share it with them and write it down in the margins of my notes.

At lunch we secured a long table seating eight or ten, and sat around it talking, with individuals in the group changing, but the talk going on, sometimes for two hours. We talked about the news, politics, music, books, poetry, film, and consciousness. I would find people talking about public events or the war or whether the use of violence was justified, talking in thoughtful and provocative ways. They raised questions about everything; they listened and responded; they had open minds. It was the highest quality of intellectual discussion I had ever known.

Their whole world interested them, from the architecture of their college buildings to the paintings in the art gallery to classical music to the way a black-light poster could cause a magical effect in their rooms. Nobody seemed bored or lacking in something to do. Nobody seemed to need to escape into numbness for relief from the world. The talk would linger long after the dishes were cleared. On a few occasions I remember spending the entire three hours from breakfast until lunch sitting in the dining hall with one or two students who ignored their classes and talked about Marx's theory of alienation or a modern novel they had been reading in class, sipping coffee all morning and finally breaking up when the lunchtime tide began to fill the dining hall.

I was continually amazed that the students recognized so many of the threats to American democracy that I had been writing about with little or no effect. They were sensitive to the misuse of governmental power, the disregarding of constitutional liberties, the depersonalization of large bureaucratic institutions, the assault on the natural environment, the inhuman senselessness of the Vietnam war. They did not get this sensitivity from me or from studying law or government. They got it from their newly expanded awareness of human values.

A large number of students considered me their friend, a family member who could be asked for help with a personal problem, an ally in the great revolution that was taking place. I was never alone, except by choice.

Students wanted me to come to their rooms and see a poster or hear a record or stare out of the window at some never-before-noticed sight or meet a friend. I was seemingly the only older person who was willing to share all their marvelous new discoveries. Yale was overflowing with people who wanted to share. They could share a meal, a walk. But this was not because they were especially gifted at relationships or closeness. It was because their abundance of discoveries led to an abundance of sharing and love. I was a happy beneficiary of this wealth.

It is beautiful when a teacher who is forty and engaged in teaching youth can also begin learning from them. A much deeper relationship springs up. I might stop by a student's room and ask if he would listen to a new record album with me, talk about it afterwards, and possibly write out the lyrics to the songs. Or I might ask another student in the dining hall if I could listen when he played his electric guitar. Still others I would ask to tell me about how to view movies or television or the news in a new way. I openly made my student friends see that they were my university, and their new knowledge was my curriculum.

At home I often felt happy and fulfilled. Sometimes a student would come out in the evening for a few hours of listening to records, talking, smoking marijuana, and eating snacks. These visits were casual, yet special. Often the students were very personal, the two of us sitting opposite one another on the floor. Those evenings left me with a glow of warmth inside, so that I went off to sleep peacefully.

There was another kind of evening when I would stop by one of several rooms in Ezra Stiles College or Morse College where I knew there would be a group of students gathered for the purpose of idly passing the time and possibly having fun. This was a wholly new kind of acceptance for me—acceptance by a group of pleasure-seekers. The conversation did not swing over to me but remained as before. And I was relieved to feel no need to say anything at all. Sometimes we just laughed a lot together. In one room at Morse College, the television was almost always on, but with the sound turned off and some rock music playing. A group of five or six sat entranced by the TV screen. The announcers and commercials seemed absurd. The world looked so serious, so ridiculous, through our eyes. People drifted in and out of the room. I was just passing time, but that was another breakthrough for me.

For a long time I hesitated about marijuana, feeling that my position forbade me to do anything illegal. But I asked the students to tell me all about it. What did it feel like, what could you do with it, what could you learn from it? And when they kept saying try it, it became harder and harder to say no. The first couple of times I smoked (after a small amount of plotting by students), nothing happened. Then I had to ask the students to teach me how to smoke marijuana and what one could feel and see.

Smoking marijuana for the first time was a profound experience in those days. It was a real gateway. There was a slowing down. It was possible to concentrate, to see and hear things more clearly. Music became an experience of interior depths and new dimensions. Ordinary things like a vegetable or the weather were seen and felt and tasted with total freshness, as if they had never been experienced before. Barriers came down. People who hardly knew each other felt at ease, felt intimate, found themselves laughing and inventing fun. Directness and honesty were possible. Communication could occur without words, and was often a very spiritual experience. Passing a joint or pipe around a circle of people, feeling both the danger of violating the law and the excitement of unknown adventure, was a ritual often done with reverence.

Out of these shared experiences of teaching and learning I began to have a new kind of relationship with students who had become my friends. I allowed myself to become vulnerable to them. I depended on them for company and fun and support. For nearly a year I worked in a vacant student room in the tower of Ezra Stiles College. This gave me a sense of security because of the close proximity of other people, and allowed the students to see that I needed this.

There was a valuable exchange of talents. A student who was a varsity swimmer would give me swimming lessons at the pool. A student who was a classical musician would offer to go with me to a concert. A movie buff would tell me about something special at the Yale cinema.

There was a true economy of youth and age. There was so much we could give each other, once the barriers were down. Their youth, enthusiasm and warmth made me feel appreciated, protected and loved, allowing me to give more and more to them. They saw values in me that I could no longer see for myself. My life was filled with friendships for the first time. In a very real sense I felt that the students had saved me. They had rescued me, the battered rebel, and taken me with them.

I would sit at a small table on the balcony of the Ezra Stiles dining hall with a look of concentration on my face, surrounded by paper and pencils. Two smiling people would come up on either side of me and say, "We thought we'd sit down and make you feel good for a few minutes, and then you can go back to work."

My closeness to students was very radical for a professor at Yale. There was a taboo against equality, vulnerability, and intimate sharing between students and faculty. The taboo was as much the product of student attitudes as those of the faculty. There was an age taboo, a dignity taboo, an authority barrier. There were many relationships between faculty and students, but they were almost all more "professional" than mine. The line was hard to define, but I felt it. Coffee with a student was on one side of the line. But it was an ironclad rule that a professor must not act in a way that gave up his status. Lying sprawled on the lawn was on the other side.

There was an equally great stricture against anything that did not seem sufficiently intellectual. Popularity with students was suspect, as if it was based on abandoned intellectual standards. To many faculty members the students were the great unwashed. And it seemed that as an upholder of "objective" standards the faculty member should not mingle too closely with those he was required to judge.

I sensed or imagined the disapproval of administrators, faculty members, and the more conventional group of students. No one said anything to me; by liberal standards, as long as I did my job I could not be criticized or questioned. The only way in which I felt anything at all was by the fact that faculty members would pretend to ignore the unusual aspects of my life. They were very nice—like people who carefully and politely do not notice a handicapped person at dinner. But that refusal to notice was not easy on me. I felt like a person who had strayed and was being subtly urged to return to the fold. This gave my educational ideas no stature. I felt that I was not regarded as a person with a definite educational philosophy which could be weighed against prevailing philosophies. Thus there was always an uncomfortable and defensive side to my life at Yale.

Far more than during the two months at Berkeley, my new life at Yale changed me as a person. For the first time I felt at ease, funny, and confident around people. I grew far less self-conscious. I made fewer plans. If I had nothing to do, I strolled down to the campus and never failed to find some people and some fun. I could take more initiatives, introducing myself and beginning conversations and relationships.

In some miraculous way a secret part of myself came into being which I had always known about but never thought could emerge with other people. This was a person who got excited and intense and happy over so many things, and angry and passionate and idealistic and yearning about other things. I was the boy jumping up and down with excitement because they had opened a new wing at the Museum of National History.

This new self within influenced me to turn a projected book that was to be about what was wrong with our society into *The Greening of America*. It started as one book, and ended as another. I began to write about the collapse of institutions and laws, but ended by writing about the hopefulness of new consciousness. A book about social disintegration became a book about human change. I saw it as my gift to the Yale students, and to their generation.

I wrote the book at Yale, in this way. I would take my writing materials to the dining halls or the library and enjoy the nearby presence of students. When they came over to my table to see me, I would talk about what I was working on, and let them feed ideas and discoveries into me. They made a huge contribution to my thinking. When it was late afternoon and I was too tired to write any longer, some students would usually find me and take me off for music and relaxation and dinner. I felt that they knew I was working for them. Writing the book was a communal experience. Many of my yellow-lined pages have stains from red spaghetti sauce or rings from coffee cups.

Into my book I was able to put more of myself than I had ever shown anywhere. I mixed serious intellectual analysis with illustrations, explanations, anecdotes, and expressions of my own feelings, just as my lectures had done. It was a new form for a professor of law to use, and it made many people uncomfortable. But I had created something that was closer than ever before to being a unique expression of me, in both its strength and its weaknesses.

At the time I wrote *The Greening of America* it was not possible to see where new consciousness was heading. We did not have the necessary perspective. Now we can look back from a bit farther down the road. For just a moment I am back in Sterling Strathcona Hall on a cold, crisp blue day. The sun comes in the tall windows of the spacious, dignified old lecture room. There are ten minutes left in the hour . . .

In the late 1960's, there was a revolution in this country, a revolution in our ways of thinking. It went much deeper than any overthrow of ruling power. This revolution changed our ideas, our philosophy, our perspective. It changed *us*.

The revolution continues to unfold today. In many ways it has already become the mainstream; in other ways it is only now beginning to touch our lives. Its impact has been felt from politics to economics to personal life.

In every area our ways of thought were radically questioned. We saw there could be new choices, possibilities, alternatives.

We had assumed that our society made sense, was doing well, knew its own direction. On the contrary, said new consciousness, many of our basic premises are false. We do not necessarily know what is right or important, or even what is happening to us. Our materialistic values and artificial products are not necessarily healthy. We do not have unlimited resources. We are living without sufficient awareness.

Established institutions and authority could no longer be depended on for guidance. It was seen that people must take greater power and give up less to organized society. All of the people must have a voice. There was a renewal of the democratic spirit.

The ills of our political and economic system became apparent to many people, and its irrationality recognized. Law and government were denied automatic respect and seen as potentially or actually harmful to individuals. The concept of an elite who must run the country was increasingly rejected.

Direct political action, direct pressure on government, refusal to obey the law, and other forms of rebellion became more common. The Vietnam war demonstrated to many people that they must maintain an individual power of conscience that could not be trusted to government, and act upon their individual conscience when necessary.

In every type of institution, from high school teams to universities to large corporations, authority was questioned and the institution's way of doing things attacked, and people called for a larger share of power for themselves.

People who had been considered by society to have virtually no rights at all, such as inmates of mental institutions and prisons, hospital patients, soldiers in the army, were seen to have rights despite their situation.

There were fundamental changes in economic values and priorities. Material wealth, security, status, competition, and power were reduced in importance. Growth, happiness, naturalness, and ecology assumed greater importance. These changes were reflected first in consumer preferences and later in political action.

Emphasis shifted from the accumulation and possession of material goods toward the most economical and imaginative and socially desirable *use* of products, exemplified by sharing.

Work was subjected to reexamination for its physical and psychological harm to the individual, as well as for its ability to provide not only a source of income, but also personal fulfillment, meaning, and happiness.

Education was conceived as an essential lifelong concern, not as a commodity or as something that takes place only in youth. The country's educational system was deeply questioned, and a search began for new educational forms and new kinds of learning.

A sense of the human community, and of its place in a larger natural community, developed. A renewed respect for human life was accompanied by a new respect for other forms of life and for the balance of nature. The environmental movement was born out of this awareness. People began to live more simply, and in accordance with nature.

People turned toward experiences of artistic, aesthetic, sensual, natural, and spiritual content. There was a growth of spiritual awareness apart from organized churchgoing, and an interest in mysticism, magic, and Eastern religions with their concept of the unity of all things.

New consciousness implied a set of social ethics, allowing us to act differently and value things differently. We need not feel obliged to participate in any business or institution that is harmful. We need not destroy the environment or living things in the course of our work or daily lives. We need not be insensitive to each other's feelings. We could treat people, including children, as equals, not as superior or inferior beings. Above all, we need never feel that our "duty" requires us to violate ourselves.

It no longer seemed valid behavior to give the appearance of total competence, control, and self-assurance at every moment. To be constantly "big" in this way was neither attractive nor likely to inspire confidence. If you were "big" all the time in an absurd world, you were simply not dealing with the absurdity.

All of these changes required that individuals take more responsibility for their own lives. The individual could be the judge of his or her own happiness. People could discover more about their own needs, their own potential.

The need for basic changes in men's and women's roles became apparent, and more impetus was given to women's liberation and to a reconsideration of the competitive, male role.

People received permission to begin recovering the child inside themselves. Many of the light-hearted aspects of new consciousness could be recognized as an expression of the child.

As ways of thinking changed, it became necessary for our ways of communicating with each other to change equally radically and rapidly. On the personal level, there was a need for much greater honesty and accuracy, especially where feelings were concerned. Concealment, pretense, façades were something we could no longer afford.

It became important to be able to communicate quickly to a great many people, and to say much in a short interval. Almost the entire culture of the late sixties had to do with new means of communication. It was a vital development in a society where recognized means of communication, especially official ones, could no longer be counted on to produce the truth.

The late sixties reminded us that we ourselves were still part of evolution. Consciousness, or awareness, or our ways of thinking, are subject to evolution just as our physical bodies are subject to evolution. One stage of awareness is succeeded by another and another, just as the early forms of life were succeeded by later adaptations.

New consciousness showed that it is possible for us to change, and that change could sometimes be necessary for survival. Therefore one of the most important consequences of new consciousness was the ethic of personal growth. Everyone had the right and the duty to grow and to change as part of our continuing evolution on the planet.

The new consciousness revolution restored direction, and knowledge of the human cause—that the growth of people is what matters, rather than any form of material "progress." Growth gave us a reason to be together, for to grow, we all need help. There was a sense of Us, We, The Movement, We the People.

The new consciousness revolution altered radically our perspective on our own lives and our country. Previously there had been a growing but unjustified reliance by people on organizational society for direction, for answers, for the promise of life. People felt steadily less powerful, seeking merely to fit into the larger system as successfully as they could, without questioning it deeply. The late sixties era gave us permission to see life in very different terms. While America was a place, a land, history, people, institutions, a country—it was not something to which we could blindly submit.

We had gone too far toward seeing society as a machine and reducing ourselves to being parts of the machine. The revolution asked us to see human society in more organic terms. We were larger in dimension, more important as a source of truth. Human intuition, feelings, conscience, values, imagination would make a larger contribution to how we lived.

We could find love for ourselves and for America again. There was somewhere magical and idealistic toward which we could travel, other than the sterile, materialistic and mechanical fate we had feared lay ahead. We could find it in our own country. We had replenished our faith.

Beginning in the earliest days in Berkeley I felt this sense of rebirth and rediscovery inside myself, and I will always remember how magical it was. Almost every evening in that summer of 1967, before going to bed, I took a walk from Mike Entin's apartment down Telegraph Avenue in the direction of Oakland and San Francisco. Telegraph became a wide street as it got farther away from campus, with glimpses across the Bay toward the twinkling tiny lights of San Francisco, if the fog had not come in yet. The avenue became for me the anonymous main drag of America, the street with the all-night gas stations and hamburger drive-ins and miniature golf and late-night liquor stores. It might have been in Arizona or Oregon, Seattle or Grand Junction, Colorado, but with the sense of adventure provided by darkness, space and distance, hills to the left, the fresh salty air from the Bay, the sea far off to the right.

Oh, do you see how it is? I can be anything I want to be. I can go to an all-night café in Oakland, and sit there with people unlike any I have known before. I can discover the San Francisco of Jack London and Charlie Chan and the foghorns. I can find a job unlike anything before—a clerk in a warehouse, a short-order cook, a salesman in an Army-Navy store. Whatever I do, it can be real. My work, my services, my friends, all can be real. The professorship at Yale, the approval of the faculty, the positions gained through recommendations and grades and tests and years of education and being so "good," so "responsible," they will not be there to obscure the truth.

And whatever is real about America—its sounds and smells, trucks, cars, bridges, its speed and crowds and excitement, its luxury and incongruity, its high culture, its pop culture, its music and books, its mountains and beaches—all of it will be mine, not as it used to be, with me as a tourist traveling to see a distant place or visit a museum, but mine because I will be open to it; I will be turned toward it, I will let it come to me, I will open the valves and ducts in me and be open to it all, and I will let it fill me and touch me and hold me, and I will be a part of it. I can rediscover America and I can rediscover myself.

And if I got this far down the avenue, if I left my position and security behind me, then maybe I could be a writer. And being a writer would mean so many things to me that they come all in a rush. To do work that meant being oneself. It meant being a thinker and even a philosopher, exploring and loving—a quiet calm person who was open to life, open to all the influences and experiences that came his way.

But being a writer is greater than this. For me it is being alive, alive as I have never been but now know that I can be. It is my version of the rediscovery of life in Berkeley, June–July 1967, and Yale, 1968–1970.

We all had to learn. We had to begin again, we had to make mistakes, follow blind alleys, experience pain and misery. Many people were lost on the way. Mike Entin died in a crash of a small plane he was piloting. Others felt despair. But what mattered was that we had seen the vision.

Yes, the vision. Eric Burdon singing about strobe lights on a warm San Francisco night. Mike once said a San Francisco night was always cool, so he thought this song must mean that the warmth came from loving somebody and being loved. And that other song—"If you're going to San Francisco, be sure to wear some flowers in your hair." The kids—oh, they are older now, but they were the first to see it. The first to see it and rejoice and show us all. The new community, the happy panel truck, the posters and music and outdoor concerts, the green corduroy jeans and beads and floppy hats. The Bay and hills and ocean and sun in the west. The red sky after sunset, the warm sea-smelling nights, the darkness and the space, the fog and fresh cool air, the far-off twinkling tiny lights.

Starting
from
Clement
Street

Four

When you are about to cross boundaries into the unknown, with many possible hardships and new experiences ahead, it is sometimes best to pause a moment at a place that is comfortable and reassuring. I arrived in San Francisco in December, 1971, for a six-month leave of absence from Yale. After the plane trip I went to the Mark Hopkins Hotel and rented a luxurious room with a view of the city.

My life at Yale was drastically changed following the publication of *The Greening of America* in the fall of 1970. I had calls, letters, invitations, interviews, photographs. Being a celebrity came at a time when the students were starting to retreat from new consciousness into a period of concern with achievement and career security, rejecting the values of the late sixties. This circumstance changed my relationship with the students from one of mutuality to one in which skepticism and even cynicism came between us.

And I felt equally uncomfortable with my public role outside of Yale. Being a celebrity meant having my days and nights filled with unceasing demands, questions, attacks, interruptions. There were many requests for lectures and articles repeating the substance of my book, but I saw no point in this when I could not yet describe the next steps forward. I had to do more learning and thinking before I had anything new to say; all I could be was a scapegoat for people's doubts.

Many people, especially intellectuals, dealt with *The Greening of America* by not taking it seriously, and seeing it as a naïve report on a passing fad. The change in the outward appearance of new consciousness in the early seventies led many people to think it had ceased to exist, or perhaps never did exist. How could I explain, either to students or to the public, that new consciousness had entered a stage of inwardness when I did not yet know this myself?

I felt the world silently changing. It seemed as if smiles were gone. The people who had looked so beautiful were gone. The people who had looked joyous and full of life were gone. The people who had looked strong and confident were gone. It was as if a psychological depression had come over the entire populace. Everywhere I encountered people marked by a sense of futility, cynicism, withdrawal, fear, and despair. I felt that people were relinquishing themselves to a hopeless fate which insisted that everything has been tried, everything is getting worse, life is on a downward track.

It seemed to me that people disappeared in the middle of friendships, or started toward others and never got there, unable to maintain contact. Something kept us from banding together to combat the despair of the times. Like others I seemed destined to face it alone.

It made me think that an oppressive atmosphere such as that of the fifties had returned, and was now overwhelming everyone, even the college students who had been my main support. I felt trapped: there was nowhere to go and no one to see or share anything with. Washington, D.C., in the 1950's had been suffocating, but it did not have the sense of eerie invasion by an unseen enemy.

Wherever I went, I felt that no eyes would meet mine. The lack of trust seemed to be everywhere. The world was becoming savage.

At the same time I was losing my ability to feel and be moved by the sources of happiness I had always relied on, such as travel and nature. I could not feel anything if I had to endure a stifling traffic jam to get there or a disagreeable lunch at a crowded and rushed place along the freeway. I could not feel history or patriotism if commercialism brazenly tried to profit from my feelings.

No matter how bad I felt elsewhere I had always been able to count on my experiences in nature. And nineteenth-century American landscape painting told me that many Americans had once been able to feel as I did, finding contentment in views of valleys, lakes, hills and Western desert mountains suffused with mystery, wonder, beyondness and inner light. But in a forest of trees reduced to stumps by power saws and with the carpet of earth mangled by the tracks of bulldozers, nature had no power to reach me. Nor could I feel free in a national forest campsite with supervision and regulation intruding everywhere. Our mechanized version of nature could no longer be trusted with my deepest feelings. In the Adirondacks and also in the

Pacific Northwest, two of my most sacred places, the government began to fly supersonic training flights over the deepest areas of wilderness, while insisting that it was doing nothing to disturb the wild. When I went to those places I would be looking for silence and the sounds of nature. And if I was to be moved by them I would have to make myself a hundred times more sensitive, so that the ordinary deafness necessary in a clanging city could be replaced by an awareness of the sound of wind in a high mountain tree or the slapping of ripples against a rock on the shore of a pond. And while I was so vulnerable I could be totally devastated by the thunderous crash of an unexpected sonic boom.

Thus it was that although in 1971 I had achieved external success, an inner voice told me that my world was actually narrowing and becoming more desolate, and that I felt profoundly unhappy. On soft balmy spring days, my body's cells would be summoned to painful far-off yearnings.

I felt a yearning and need to become a better organism. I felt slow and sluggish and overcomplicated. I wanted to live a simpler way, to be more in touch with the realities of a city, to be closer to nature, to be equal with other people. I wanted to be independent, self-reliant, centered. My life of classes, meetings, papers, and schedules seemed so complicated, so unsatisfying, so unnecessary. I wanted to play hookey from having to be in the class of "the best." I had always been "special"—a lawyer, a professor, a celebrity; this was supposed to be "better" than not being special— "better" in the sense of superior, at least in my mythology. But my life in Washington, and even more so at Yale, had been too refined. It was hard to get a feeling of self-reliance and self-sufficiency, as I had become increasingly pampered and therefore out of touch. For ten academic years I had been virtually cut off from whatever was happening in the outside world; I knew only students, libraries, dormitories, classrooms. I had lived in one narrow corridor of life. Meanwhile, what had become of the rest of the world? What had people learned that I did not know?

I felt I was a person whose public life had been achieved at the price of an ecological disaster within, a career based on neglect of my own needs. I had promised myself that when *The Greening of America* was finished, I would give full priority to looking after my own life. If I did not now keep the bargain I had made with myself in order to work so single-mindedly on the book, it would have been an act of self-betrayal. This was all felt instinctually, organically.

There was also a second voice that questioned the validity of my success. It said, you are falling behind—the position of your own class, the liberal intellectuals, has been seriously compromised. To be a liberal intellectual, I felt, was to be trapped in a situation where the growth of one's mind and knowledge would be nearly impossible. The intellectual was out of touch with popular culture such as rock music and television. I felt little connection to "ordinary people." The intellectual was supposed to keep up a tough, wisecracking, competitive façade, showing no pain or smallness. The intellectual's friendships seemed lacking in closeness, intimacy, or the willingness to experiment. Moving in such a limited reality, I felt that I might easily miss the essential truths while building logical arguments. We intellectuals had denied stature to the new while having no new approaches of our own. We felt threatened. We could become the forces of reaction, the McCarthyites of the seventies, unless we could find a way forward.

And then my secure position as a tenured professor was suddenly threatened from within by repressed sensual forces. It happened this way.

On two different occasions I had an unsettling experience with separate students. We would play records and talk. Neither was a student I felt especially close to. But for some reason, each spoke up on a subject that I had never broached before with a student. Each asked me what I knew about my own sexual feelings.

Tom and I were sitting close together; I was silent, and he asked me what I was feeling. Obviously he sensed something unspoken in the atmosphere, and wanted me to acknowledge it. I refused. Feeling threatened, I remained silent. Then I said, "You tell me," so that if I was wrong about what I feared he was thinking, I would not give myself away. In a very gentle and reassuring way he said, "I think you are homosexual and are attracted to me." "Yes," I admitted, petrified. "That's okay, I just wanted to tell you that I am aware of your feelings," he said, holding my hand. "I don't want to pursue those feelings myself," he continued, "although I have felt them too. But shouldn't you learn more about yourself?"

Benjamin's message was delivered in a very different style. He had come to see me several times before, and enjoyed showing me visual and acoustical magic. This time he was showing me shadows on the wall, and using his hands to project them. He asked me to do the same. Then his shadow asked my shadow to dance. "Look only at the wall, not at my hands," he said. The dancers met and twined together. I felt forbidden pleasure. It was permitted to the shadows, the ballet dancers on the wall. I did not look around to acknowledge that Benjamin and I were gently touching each other and holding hands.

I felt scared, for this was not mere conversation. Something was really happening. Again I was cautious. "What do you think we are feeling?" I asked Benjamin. And then he said much the same thing as Tom. Except that Benjamin said it with a magician's smile.

These two messengers shook my Yale self to its depths. If these two could see, everyone could see. I could not really hide any more, certainly not from myself. And the warmth between us, though brief, had felt so good. I decided I must have space to think. For the first time ever I canceled my classes for a week, and flew out to San Francisco.

Cut the bullshit, Charles, I told myself. Even the prudent, rational, clear side of myself said that I must answer the questions. At age forty-three, it could hardly be imprudent to learn the truth about myself. If not now, when?

Suddenly I wanted to be nineteen and gay and on my own in the city, away from home and school for the first time. I wanted an apartment of my own, in a city where nobody knew me. I wanted to have no obligations, have all of my senses ready for any adventure that came my way. I desperately wanted and yearned for the adolescence I felt I had missed.

All of this came together in a fantasy: an imaginary apartment in San Francisco near Clement Street. The Clement Street neighborhood seemed to give permission for my fantasy. Clement Street is in the Richmond District, in the western part of the city where there is a sense of space and quiet, frequent fog and the almost visible influence of the ocean. Clement Street itself is a long shopping street with many small, very good restaurants and stores. The marvelous thing about Clement Street is its variety, a variety deeply rooted in ethnic populations but with the addition of San Francisco uniqueness and a scattering of young people.

Somewhere near Clement Street, on one of the quiet, uncluttered cross-streets that are called avenues, I dreamed I had a sunny kitchen looking over a green backyard, and a front bedroom that could be sensual and exotic. And then I was struck with a realization: I could actually do it. In this apartment, without the presence of anyone from the past, I could be free.

Back at Yale after my week's trip, I was filled with doubts and anxieties. But I had to take the chance that I could discover a person within me whom I did not even know where to look for. And if this person had a chance of surviving, then for the first time I would have an exhilarating but terrifying choice. There would be another life available to me, away from my secure Yale self. Would this new life be happier? Could I give up what I already had? These questions were utterly beyond me, for I had not yet tried living in the imaginary apartment.

I had no idea that I was beginning a search that others were also making; I believed that my situation, my problems, and my decisions were unique. I did not see that other human beings would also be responding to forces much larger than any person's individual life, forces such as the falling off of nurture and the need to seek new knowledge and new sources of energy and strength. Thus I started out on a pathway for reasons that seemed entirely my own, but actually took part in a much greater human transformation.

I had no way of knowing that I was asking myself

an evolutionary question. I did not know that I would be seeking to change myself fundamentally; I could not have imagined that the search I was about to begin would go so deep. We cannot be expected to know what it would feel like to be propelled toward the next stage of evolution.

What pushes us toward an evolutionary step is unbearable pain and deprivation in our present lives. As long as we accept this pain, we do not change. We say that our bad feelings are due to our own failures; they are "us." But finally there comes a moment when we must escape. We change perspective and no longer accept the pain as bearable, but instead see that it has a cause, and survival requires that we get away. We acknowledge the existence of our pain but reject its necessity. This is the moment of evolutionary rebellion.

Evolutionary rebellion is a refusal, born of utmost necessity, to continue to believe in things the way they are. It is a moment of saying, there may be something out there that we do not know but must search for, because we cannot remain where we are. We finally accept and yield to what our pain and our yearnings tell us. We dismiss the ego, and yield to nature and the universe. I would return to San Francisco.

Out of my twenty years of loneliness, my unfilled desires, my torment, a new voice spoke in utmost quiet.

I rebel.

I will endure this no longer. The pain is greater than nature intended me to bear. I must cease to accept this, and begin to hunt for something better. I am leaving.

Be not content, Charles. Do not accept this system of things.

Do not believe it, do not pass it on. Do not allow your life to stop here, in the desert.

Seek.

From my room at the Mark Hopkins, with the fall term at Yale behind me and six months of freedom ahead, the city of San Francisco at night gleamed with possibilities. Going down the streets in the darkness, I saw the lighted windows as a series of openings to worlds beyond. Walking or riding in a car, I could catch a glimpse into apartments nearby, the windows often inviting with stained glass, plants, and Victorian shapes. In the distance, far down the avenues, on the hills, thousands of other windows beckoned.

I located an apartment on Russian Hill, a furnished flat, with an antique gas heater and rear windows that looked over the city rooftops. It would serve as a real-life setting for my fantasy. The very first night in my new home, eating alone and looking out over the city, I felt a surge of excitement at my freedom. The city streets stretched in every direction, hinting at adventures and the unknown. I immediately felt totally anonymous. I was a young man free in the city. I remembered my life in Washington, D.C., at the Wilshire Crescent, and I realized that now I had a second chance. If I stepped outside this new apartment into the city, perhaps on a night with a misty winter rain falling, there could be a fresh beginning, and any street or avenue could lead somewhere I had never been before.

I began to explore the gay subculture of San Francisco. I met gay people, young and old, went to a gay sex film (I had never before seen any sort of pornographic film), looked at gay publications and magazines. For the first time in my life, I was looking at photographs of young men who were openly meant to be seen as desirable objects. I noticed a photograph of Kent, a blond kid who was advertised as a "model"—a young man who offered sex for hire.

The first new experience I tried was "cruising." Cruising is defined by *Webster's New Collegiate Dictionary* as, "to go about the streets, at random, but on the lookout for possible developments." Always before, my look had said, "Hello, nice to meet you. Please keep your distance." Now, if I passed a young man lounging in front of a store on Hyde Street, my look said: "I might like something to happen between us." Every block of the city took on excitement and meaning. I did not know who was gay and who was not. Men I glanced at stared back at me in a wholly new way. Usually their expressions said, "I see you, and I don't want your attention." A few men were curious, but that was all.

In truth my "cruising" was not quite real: I did not seriously attempt to pick anyone up. I did not have a clear idea of what would happen if someone returned my glance and we ended up at his or my apartment. In fact I had never once pictured sex of any kind between men. My fantasies concerned warm embraces, not nakedness, and never, *never* genitals, male or female. Genitals, I thought, were hairy, smelly, unappetizing. I could not speak the word "penis" or "vagina." And without a picture in my head of what to do if I ever found myself alone with a gay man, I had a terrifying fear that any sexual encounter would cause me to freeze in awkwardness and embarrassment.

I decided to attend San Francisco Gay Rap, a weekly open meeting. Walking alone down Pine Street toward Laguna required all my courage. All my life I had enjoyed the privileged status of a heterosexual man with everyone I knew, however little I actually was entitled to it. I felt that this one step would label me homosexual forever. Whatever happened, there would be no taking it back.

I nervously climbed some steps to a building called Alternative Futures Commune, where Gay Rap was held. I found myself in a large bare room with maybe fifty males of various ages, almost all in blue jeans or work clothes. After some routine announcements came twenty minutes of "sensitivity exercises" in which the men were encouraged to touch each other and to loosen up their bodies. I stood ill at ease on the sidelines.

Then we broke up into small groups for what proved to be rambling, hesitant, leaderless discussions. Everyone looked strange and uncomfortable. It was all so cheerless and depressing. No one appeared attractive. They seemed resigned and burdened with self-hatred. In my group there were only one or two young men I could imagine a faint chance of liking. I kept asking myself whether it was really true that this was my new peer group, the people I had most in common with. In my new existence, maybe they were.

I would be invited to a Victorian house where three or four people lived, sometimes for a quiet visit, sometimes for a party. The household felt unstructured and exotic, with immediate easy warmth and touching. There was a far more permissive informality than I had known: one could sit in a corner and not talk or relate to anyone, or watch a pair of bleary-eyed lovers casually emerge from a bedroom, without there being any need to take special notice. The people were mostly young and long-haired. There were many signs of interest in the occult or some sort of spiritual awakening. Something indefinable held people together, and reached out to include me as well, almost as soon as I entered. We were a ragged band of searchers, refugees from some other place, the people who couldn't fit in.

Two weeks passed quickly, with so much to see and learn about. As the end of the year approached, I began to get impatient with myself. I was avoiding the real issue. I had not come to San Francisco to study the gay scene as a sociologist, or to meet new people in order to be sociable. The immense barrier in front of me was sex. It was time for it to happen.

I imperatively felt that I must take a decisive step before the new year. Finally it was the last day before New Year's Eve. It was time to ACT. There is a moment you have to watch for, when preparations for a much-feared new experience or departure are complete, and any further delay or evasion may prove to be a permanent giving up. *If you believe, leap.* Trust there is a safe landing on the other side.

There was a hysterical parent in me who desperately wanted me to rethink everything. But I had done my thinking long before. My new anonymous freedom would not last much longer; soon I might walk into my apartment and find the hysterical parent waiting for me, and it would all be over. Be cool, be the Expedition Leader, I told myself. Act.

I got out the photo of the "model" that I had admired, picked up the phone, and dialed the number. A voice answered and I asked for Kent. "Yes, this is Kent." He took my call very easily. "Sure, I will be over in half an hour," he said.

I had set it in motion. My excitement and exuberance grew as the minutes flew by.

When the bell rang, I held my breath and opened the door. My senses were totally alert, my feelings absolutely frozen. There was a polite blond young man of about twenty. His hand felt soft and there was a surprising freshness to him, as if he had just come from a shower. He apologized for being a bit late. His respectful manner made me feel a bit easier.

We sat down on the couch. "There's something I've got to explain to you," I said in my professorial manner. "This may be hard to believe, but I don't know what sex is like or what to do. It's something I want to try, however. It's important for me to try it, I've made up my mind. Whatever happens will be fine with me. I don't know if I will feel anything. Are you comfortable with this situation? If not, maybe we can just talk. Here, is it all right if I hold your hand?"

I let him feel my trembling hand. He held it softly and gently. No one had held me in this way since I was a child.

We talked a little. He liked the beach. He had an easy life, he said. Many interesting people, lots of free time. "Do you feel less anxious now?" he said.

"Could we go into the bedroom and take our clothes off?" I bravely asked. "I would like to know how that feels." He shed his clothes easily, no underwear beneath his jeans. His body was beautiful. My feelings stirred. "Let's lie down next to each other," I suggested, still intrepid. "Show me what people do."

He touched me and rubbed me softly and gently. I relaxed into the feelings he gave me. He was detached but easy and reassuring, even sweet. I relaxed still more. He put his hand on my penis. I would have expected to flinch and shudder at this totally unheard of, forbidden, unthinkable action. But it was a most beautiful feeling.

I was filled with awe and wonder that one person could make another person feel so good. The pure floating beauty of how he was making me feel seemed truly spiritual. What a miracle that another person, a person I did not even know, a person I was paying, could make me feel like that; it was a gift from the gods. From the gods, from this young man.

He put his mouth around my penis, and I accepted that, and it made the sunlight flooding into me still brighter, the dark mysterious spaces opening up still more magical. And then, in what felt like the first purely instinctual, wholly natural act of my life, I turned and opened my mouth to his penis, and instead of the utter repulsion I would have expected, I felt unknown pleasure.

Finally we lay side by side and he held me again and quite naturally and wonderfully I had an orgasm. And with that, bells of relief and happiness rung in my head. I am all right! I can do it! I am a normal, natural, sexual being! I am not frightened and frozen, I have the power to feel. It is not so hard after all. If you relax, Nature does the work.

What a joke, what a discovery—it is so easy! How long I have been frightened when there was nothing to fear, how long I have envied others for what was in me too. Yes, I have lost thirty years. That is a bitter thought. But in some way those thirty years were all repaid by this single glorious moment. What cosmic glee and laughter swept me—to have taken a crazy chance and be able to say I was right!

I gave Kent twenty-five dollars, then ten more. "I want you to know you've changed someone's life today," I said. "I guess you have good times and bad times in your work, but today you did something good, today you did the rarest of all things and made a difference in another person's life."

He kissed me on the cheek and was gone.

In the next two weeks I called several more times, asking for other names. I made it clear to myself beyond doubt that I had crossed the line, that it was not a once-only experience. It was now part of my life.

I had very different experiences every time; that was one of the unexpected things I learned. Sex was not one thing, it was many things, as different as people were different. I had only good experiences. I asked each model to teach me something, to be my therapist, to help me overcome my fear and my ignorance.

My second visitor to the new apartment was young and denim-clad, and he was outrageous. He showed me that it was possible to be funny, to establish intimacy through humor, and that was a wonderful new freedom for me. With another model, I took the initiative of saying I would simply like to curl up and feel small, and we did not even have sex. A third was extremely soft and vulnerable, while another took a great many initiatives, showing me how to let someone else have control.

I saw the models as sexual therapists even if they did not see themselves that way. Because the gay world suffers from so much repression and outright oppression, the need for the services of models may be more understandable to both parties than in the heterosexual world. A man with a respectable job might have legitimate reasons for being unable to find sexual companionship, and a person who served this need could take pride in what he did. There was a chance for mutual respect. The model preserved his autonomy, which in many ways might be greater than the client's. I felt I was cutting through hypocritical morality.

The crucial thing that I had done with the models,

which I felt as if I had never done before, was ASK. That word was like a key, opening up a flood of new awareness. I had never *asked* for anything before. Not for affection, not for help, not for love, not for sex. And as a result nobody had made it their business to make me happy. It felt good to realize that I could ask.

I walked down to Polk Street very late one night, when the darkness, the fog, and the rain made an enclosure of my part of the city, and stood on a corner like one of those figures slouching in doorways I had seen, the shadowy, dull, hollow figures of the homosexual world, waiting for an episode of impersonal sex. The feeling I had was this: I am here, on this street of lonely people, of cruising, of pick-ups, because I was unable to fulfill a most essential need of life —a warm person to share my bed, a person to share break-fast and late-night cookies, a person who is, even if only for a night, my own. The securities of my professional life— what did any of that matter in the face of this elementary lack? A figure slouched in a doorway down the block—a young man in dirty blue jeans, possibly without accomplish-ments or education—he could give me what all of my re-spectability could not. How good it feels to stand here in this drizzle, a shabby figure in ill-fitting clothes. How good it is to shed all pride and stand here and say: I don't have anything that really matters. I'm the poorest person on this street, the ultimate beggar. I would pay that young man over there to put his arm around me. It feels so honest, so real, to experience my poverty at last. It is so good to be here standing at this corner, in this drizzle, watching the shadowy passers-by. Some great weight is off me, I feel free. To walk across the Yale campus, exchanging greetings— what a strain that was, what a lie, what a robbery of self!

Here, on this corner, I have nothing, but I have myself, and in some profound way, I am not lonely, not empty any longer.

It seemed to me at this moment that the models had been the only real thing in my life. Here I was, past midnight on Polk Street, a street of sleazy gay bars, a street of people in leather who weren't motorcycle riders, a street with a sex bookshop at one end and a sex cinema at the other, a street with the darkest poetry of the city. I liked the feeling of humility, of honesty, of basicness that Polk Street gave me. This was the street where sham ended, where self-deception ended, where all the politeness and pretenses ended. Down, down, down and dirty—but true.

I can make it in this world, I told myself. I can survive. I am not dependent on that other world. I am freer than I thought. I climbed the quiet foggy streets back to my new home.

Early in February my spirits came crashing down. It began when the police vice squad started arresting the models and I too was involved. I was visiting a so-called model agency, expecting to look at their book of photographs prior to telephoning one last model. Instead, the police were there.

"Is this a raid?" I asked. They wanted to know who I was. While I was showing them my identification, I told the police officers how much I resented their intrusion into my private life. They replied by asking if I would testify against the models. "I would never do that, they have done me a lot of good," I said. "This place fills a real need for some gay men. The models have told me they are models by choice. What is the crime and where is the victim? I don't think you are doing society any good by this raid, and I certainly won't help you." At this point, since they no longer showed any interest in me, I walked out.

Back at my apartment my hysterical self took over, in waves of anxiety, fear of exposure and disgrace. I felt the first signs of an overwhelming depression.

Some days later I drove over to Berkeley for what was advertised as a social event for gay people. I found my way to a campus building, feeling very self-conscious and totally out of place. There were a few quite ill-at-ease college-age kids not looking at me or at each other, and a man in charge who was the sympathetic college-chaplain type. I sat on a couch for a while, feeling like a professional man in his forties at a college mixer, ogling the sweet young people with some dark, sinister purpose. What am I doing here? I cried inside myself. How low I have fallen, a depraved law professor at a teenage church social, a dark menacing presence among the pure youngsters, a middle-aged person compulsively driven to self-destruction. I bolted from the room and fled back in the darkness toward the safety of my car.

The sights and experiences of the last month and a half all began to seem horribly bizarre, part of some nightmare world, far from the clean rational secure position that had been mine at Yale. Male prostitutes. Boys dancing with boys. Older men walking the streets with hungry, predatory looks, as if they had no interests or work or comforts except the raw, glittering need for sex. What had once seemed exciting now felt like some excessively strange foreign food that would turn the stomach: smells of exotic oils and incense, screeching music in gay bars, hysterically dressed young men with purple fingernail polish.

I said to myself, it's been too hard, it's been too weird,

I've pushed myself too far. I want to go home and feel safe. I want to cover myself up with blankets and hide. I've done enough, been brave enough, taken enough risks, and now I want to be small.

When I got back to my apartment, I rushed for the bed and rolled up in the blankets and stayed there like a child in hiding, with just a peephole in the blankets to breathe through, breathing as if I had run miles and miles through the terrifying night.

The child! Suddenly I recognized the child within me, the child I never let anybody see—the small, frightened, sad, panicky, abandoned, needy child. And I felt an intense desire to show this child to other people, to be a dependent person that needed to be soothed and cuddled and held and reassured. I wanted a big person to take care of me.

I had always tried to cover up that frightened, whimpering, clinging, small person within me. I felt it was a disgrace, a secret that would shock the lawyers or professors that I knew. Even my best friends would feel embarrassed and uncomfortable.

Now I instinctively wanted this small person to return. How much I had missed him. How lonely and strange it had been, out in the world without him. Only very slowly did I realize that this recovery was as important as finding the sexual being within me.

February 21, 1972, was a day I will never forget. I woke up in the morning feeling fearful, anxious, and insecure. For a long time I remained in the big bed facing the window, staring out over the city. It was four days after the visit to Berkeley. Those days had been spent almost entirely alone, feeling vulnerable and tiny. "Crack, crack, crack . . . ," began a page in my notebook. Something was cracking—my façade, my ability to hold myself together and show no needs.

I rolled a huge joint of potent marijuana and smoked it all. A silence descended. I was transported more deeply into myself than I had ever gone before. Fearing the phone or the slightest interruption of my trance, I walked outside. Something in me had decided not to fight the feelings any longer. Instead, I would go toward them. I would plunge into my fears. Somehow, it would be better. I climbed the stone steps across from my house and sat there in the bright sun for hours, high above the street, and let the thoughts come.

Awnings, my first thought was of awnings. Why? Then I remembered the long forgotten awnings on my childhood bedroom window. And my position on the steps recalled the feeling looking down at the street from the window of our apartment on West 82nd Street in New York, where we lived from my early childhood until I was about ten years old.

These were no ordinary memories. They were the actual feelings, as vivid and real and immediate as when I had first felt them, stored in my mind all of these years. In my five years of psychoanalysis, I had often talked about childhood feelings, but always as a grown-up person remembering secondhand. Never had I actually felt them. Now I was granted a visit back there to 82nd Street, to a world I never imagined I could visit again, to recapture the precious buried secrets of the past.

And then the fears began to come. . . . I was so afraid of the other boys in the park . . . the boys who could do everything better than I could, and could beat me up. . . . My father, very angry and terrible, with his hat on, furious

. . . *eeeee* the bogeyman the bogeyman in the closet, I can't sleep, the bogeyman in the closet. . . . My mother and father have an ARGUMENT, a *Scene,* screaming, crying, hysterical. . . . My grandmother shouting at my father, then having an ATTACK, oh, oh the pain, Daddy angry, Daddy FURIOUS. I am to blame, everyone hates me, the bad boys hate me, Daddy hates me, I have to stay close to the Nurse, I have to stay close to Mommy, I hide in the blankets. . . . The kidnappers will kidnap me, the bad men will come and take me away, there's no one to protect me. . . . Say please, say thank you, say you're sorry, say you're sorry THIS MINUTE, DO YOU HEAR WHAT I SAID? It's all your fault, it's your fault, that's the end of that, they'll send you away, they'll SEND ME TO BOARDING SCHOOL no no no no, don't let them, don't send me away. I want my Nuggy, my blanket, I want my Nuggy. Don't send me to camp, to public school, to the hospital. . . . I can't stop carrying on —I'm like the wild man from Borneo, I want my Nuggy, I want to cuddle in the blankets with Daddy and Mommy. I want to be little, I want to be a small boy, I don't want to go to school, I don't want to go to camp, I want to stay in my own little bed with my Nuggy, all I want is to be little. . . .

Later I realized I had discovered a time machine that would allow me to set a dial, fix a lever in position, and push a button to return to any earlier place in my life. That return was true to the original, so that people, such as my father, appeared as they then looked. There would be the smells and tastes and sounds of that time as well, but more importantly, there would be the feelings I had then, both good and bad. I could feel the tension as my mother and father argued or feel the excitement of the Empire State Building lit up at night. I could become that small person again, show him to myself and to others. Perhaps that sad, frightened child could be accepted, comforted, loved as a part of me.

At the same time that I experienced these dioramas of the past, I could see myself from the outside as if I was in a film or a play. From this viewpoint I could, miraculously, reevaluate my beliefs as to what actually happened in my childhood. I could change my feelings about these scenes from the past, and consequently the present-day feelings about my parents, my brother, and myself were changed. I realized I had the power to love my parents and my brother more than I did.

Sometimes my father would come home from the office in a rage, upsetting the household and frightening me. I saw him then as a bad person, and blamed him for the unhappiness in our home. Now I could repeat the scene, hear his key in the lock of our apartment, feel the tension as he came in, watch his frowning presence disappear into the rear bedroom and look at myself tense and afraid and angry at this menacing person. But then I stepped back and saw something new. I saw that he actually wanted a lot of immediate love and attention, that none of us—my mother, my brother, me—knew how to approach him or make him smile or calm him down. We did not know that it was possible, or that we had the power to do it, or that he would have allowed it, or that he deserved our love, or that we would have felt better if we had given it, or that it would have been less emotionally expensive by far than what we actually did do—which was to withdraw—or that it might have greatly changed him, freeing him to give us more.

First I felt unbearably sad—so much unnecessary pain! The pain in our faces could have been happiness, but for our ignorance. My second feeling was a flood of compassion and love. A whole curtain of anger was pulled away. I could feel a new love for my mother and father and brother, who all were victims of what we did not know.

As I grew up, I felt a need to control the child within me, to drive away the terror and make myself able to function in the world. I said to myself, you cannot live in that world of mountains and music and adventure. You must build a career, a good reputation; you must forsake horizons for achievements, since achievements bring independence and freedom. The child is too dependent, his magic will come to nothing if he does not first become strong. Thus the child must be hidden, and a strong and capable person must be formed, going to high school, college and law school, building a position in the real world, not always happy but always surviving, until the time of the child would come round again.

And now I could see that the child in me explained the contours of the big person I showed to the world. I could begin to see how that big person had been shaped like a foam rubber coating over the tender, fragile person beneath. The whole way I dealt with the world could be understood in reference to my hidden fears and pain. It is one thing to know this in theory, as when I talked so safely to the psychoanalyst in Washington, and an entirely different thing to feel it and see it and be it.

Seeing all of this, and discovering that child still buried within me, I began to realize that the child might now become important to me. For the first time I glimpsed the idea that if I were smaller, it could be easier for me to feel a need for others and to let others see this. I had prevented people from giving me the love and support that I inwardly craved. I had hidden my child where not even the most perceptive person I knew could see it. Could I change? Instead of forever searching for someone big enough to take care of me as I was, could I become smaller, by showing other people more of my needs? Could I shrink, and thereby populate the world with bigger, calmer, more reassuring people?

The vast majority of days I spent absolutely alone. I gave myself great oceans of time and space. For I was rediscovering feelings within me that gave me surprise after surprise of happiness. They were the positive and self-loving feelings I had as a boy, and it was like meeting up with an old and most treasured friend whom I had never expected to know again. When I was a boy I could be as centered as a cat for long hours, wanting nothing but my own thoughts and feelings and activities. I could be content with a good book. Classical music held me, and old coins, and clouds. I was Captain Charles, ruler of the universe! With my chief deputy, Grand Admiral Singrass! I had a rocket ship to travel across my domain, and a magic wand to make any wish come true. I signed my decrees with a magnificent signature like that of John Hancock.

I walked around the city, evoking these boyhood feelings. I went to a little luncheon-restaurant, run by two ladies in starched white uniforms and slight German or Swedish accents, and it reminded me of nurses from long ago with names like Hilda. I sat in a Foster's cafeteria up on Geary near Clement Street with the old ladies of the neighborhood having their coffee, and it reminded me of Broadway and Eighty-sixth Street, in the neighborhood of my childhood. I went to the Russian restaurants on Clement Street and ordered myself borscht and piroshki as if my grandmother Lesinsky were taking me out to lunch. My grandfather Reich would have taken me out to the park to feed the pigeons and ducks, so I went to the pond by the Palace of Fine Arts with a loaf of stale sourdough bread for the birds. I bought a Brooks Brothers robe like my father's.

I found I could make a game of evoking feelings from any period in my life, and then seriously examining them to learn more about myself. By walking in the financial district I could feel like a young lawyer again. By sitting in the library on the campus at Berkeley I could remember the feeling of being a teacher at Yale. Wherever I went I carried a spiral notebook, and into that notebook went my thoughts. I wanted to open up my mind, to reach deeper into it than I had ever been able to before.

I tried to carry this same sense of freedom into finding a new San Francisco person within myself. There was a place that served espresso coffee and tea at the corner of Third and Clement, where I could sit without feeling hurried and look out the window toward the streets and Mount Sutro beyond, working quietly in my notebooks. There were antique stores up and down Clement Street that allowed me to begin buying small things for my apartment that fitted its old and artistic nature. There was Golden Gate Park, with the Victorian glass Conservatory of Flowers. There was Huntington Park on top of Nob Hill, a place full of pigeons, children playing on slides, and old people sitting on benches. There were new small shops where young people sold dolls or beads or plants or natural foods or spices.

Just as I had loved rain and storms all my life, I loved the magnificence of the winter rainstorms in San Francisco. First, greyness would pile up behind a southwest wind, perhaps for half a day. Then the rain would sweep in from the ocean, as fresh and sparkling as the ocean itself, and then there would be brilliant sun and blue sky, then more rain, then sun and sky again—a theater of clouds and wind and freshness that I could watch hour after hour, and feel complete and satisfied with.

One day I decided to take one of the folding chairs in the kitchen and sit outside in the sun. Thereafter, whenever I felt like it I would sit in my chair looking at the view across the Bay toward Berkeley, watching the life on the street, saying hello to my neighbors.

Virtually everything I did was an effort to make me think. I wanted to get the full meaning out of every occurrence. When there seemed to be nothing new to think about, I would continue my search. I would sit still and let thoughts come. I brought my spiral notebooks to the Mark Hopkins coffee shop, and tempted thoughts to venture into the space created by waiting for breakfast.

And as my depression finally gave way, my home became a place of delights from morning to night. For a while I did not go to see anyone or invite anyone to see me; the pleasures seemed too great for interruption. I had plants and stained glass in the windows, and I slowed down to watch leaves uncurl and reflections move. I lay in bed, watching a vintage Charlie Chan or Sherlock Holmes movie, seeing the light on top of the Mark Hopkins outside and perhaps hearing the last distant bells of the cable cars or the foghorns out in the Bay, and finally falling asleep with the television movie still on, feeling so snuggled into the blankets of the big bed. . . .

Whenever it seemed appropriate I would go to the vicinity of my imaginary apartment near Clement Street, and ask myself what progress I was making and whether my fantasy still seemed real. Almost as soon as I began doing this, I realized that there had been a hidden dimension to this fantasy all along. The Richmond neighborhood, in which Clement Street was located, triggered my childhood memories. The Richmond was like the Upper West Side of New York in the 1930's. This hidden dimension greatly added to my belief that I was on the track of real self-discovery, and that I could depend upon my own unconscious perceptions to guide me. For if Clement Street stood not only for the present but also for the past, there was further proof that the "new space" I had come to San Francisco to find lay at least in part in my own buried past, a place where my conditioned self would never have even considered looking. And yet by following the instincts of my fantasies, I had been clearly guided: Clement Street with its old Russian men over tea, elderly ladies buying groceries, borscht and Foster's English muffins . . . the road ahead lay backward through my lost self. And I, who all my life had been fascinated by the idea of secret entrances, hidden passageways, unexpected clues in mystery stories—I had found the opening, had in a certain sense known where to look—somewhere on Clement Street.

In the early spring, with my fear and depression subsiding and my life more calmly settled, I began my search for a lover. I hoped to meet a special young man who was strong, athletic, tall and lean, with a face half child, half sensual god, friendly and remote and aristocratic and funny. He would be warm, loving, and protective toward me, and teach me to be happy, free, spontaneous, sensual and brave.

I did not force myself to look for someone "appropriate," such as an artist or professional man in his forties, with a substantial career of his own. That was the course I had chosen as a young lawyer—searching for a woman who was "appropriate"—and it was a search without desire. I could not imagine intimacy with a man my own age. The thought was threatening. Sexually and emotionally, I felt as if I were a boy at puberty, just beginning to feel the stirrings of adolescence. What I desired and yearned for was a somewhat older boy. Which should I pursue—the "appropriate" or the utterly inappropriate?

I might have been cautioned that to seek a young person would be to incur a deep self-hatred. I would feel myself to be a "dirty old man" compared to virtuous clean-cut youths. I would feel my forty-three-year-old face and body were hopelessly inferior to that of the young man, and I would suffer from the insecurity of feeling less attractive than he. He would be attracted to other young men, and I would feel the pain of jealousy. He might be less support-ive and giving than I could be, and so there might be inequality.

Against these very realistic arguments, all of which soon proved to be true, I set one single idea: follow your inmost desires. I must have the integrity to look for what I wanted. I must start at the place where I could imagine intimacy, no matter how foolish and risky that was. For at all costs, I must start at a point of unquestionable authentic-ity. Perhaps that authentic point would prove to be the beginning of a long and winding trail that would finally lead to growing up emotionally and being able to be intimate with more mature men, or even women. That was at least a possibility. But if I tried to go directly to a more mature relationship, I might lose or never find the thread of authen-ticity that wound down along the trail from my childhood.

I did what I could to make my fantasy fit the minimum requirements of reality. Instead of a sixteen-year-old, I imagined someone in his twenties. To avoid too much inequality, I would look for someone to whom I could give intellectual respect. In many areas he could be my teacher, for that was something the boy in me desperately wanted. I would be his teacher in every way I could, and thereby make sure that the relationship was nurturing to him.

I was guided by two other ideals. First, the person I wanted had to be a fellow searcher like myself. I hoped for a person who held the vision of personal growth and higher consciousness. I felt that such people were my real peer group. They were the people I was attracted to. They were in some way revolutionary, and had fled from the oppressive outside society. They were explorers or idealists; they believed in magic.

The second ideal was that there must be physical closeness and intimacy, for this was the experience of which I was totally starved. I especially felt the need to be loved physically because while I had given love in this way, I had never received it. I also needed to learn how to be at ease physically with myself and with others. I was certain that for me at least, sensuality was an elemental need, and I should pursue it until I was satisfied that I had attained it.

The qualities I was looking for were hard to find in the gay world. Gay people had experienced so much oppression (and so much consequent insecurity in their relationships), that self-hatred, mistrust, and burned-out disillusionment often pervaded their lives. Damage appeared universal. Sometimes the faces in a bar or on Polk Street nearly drove me to despair, they all looked so used up by life.

But even if I could not get very far toward what I was looking for, I felt that no experience I had could possibly be a mistake as long as I was able to derive new thoughts and feelings from it. There could be no real setbacks. I could do myself no real harm. So long as I thought enough, I could only learn and grow. That fact allowed me to dare things I would not have done otherwise. My attitude was that one way or another I was going to learn something new. And over and over again this belief turned out to be true. Truth came from the most unexpected places and from the most dismal occurrences. There was no losing.

I started with what was for me a most difficult, paralyzing, frightening assignment: pick somebody up in a bar. Whenever I went to a bar, I merely stood around, felt embarrassed and frightened, and eventually went home. One Sunday night I went very early, determined to try to make something happen. I got there when the place was empty, and this allowed me to get accustomed to my surroundings, watch each person arrive, and feel as if I was the confident host, rather than an outsider trying to mingle. The plan worked; I felt at ease, and for the first time smiled and talked with people. Around midnight I started talking to a very pleasant but rather lonely-looking young man, who could have been a slightly older version of one of my students. In fact, he had been attending Berkeley, but at the moment he was taking time off from school to earn some money. We talked and he seemed to welcome my company. Finally it was 2:00 A.M., closing time, and I asked Ben if he wanted a ride anywhere. He said that would be nice, so we left together. "Where can I take you?" I asked once we were in the car. "Market Street," he said. I asked him why, since it was only two blocks away, and he said the last bus for Berkeley had already left, and he would stay in an all-night cafe until morning. I took his request at face value, but then the thought occurred to me: his plan sounds so dreary, perhaps I could persuade him to change his mind. Maybe at last I've found someone who will come home with me. With my heart in my mouth, I ventured something like this: "I have an extra bedroom—would you prefer to stay at my place?" He seemed surprised and grateful. At my apartment, I wanted him to sleep with me, but felt such an idea could hardly be broached. We had milk and cookies, and I showed him to a bed in the front room. "Why go to the trouble of fixing up an extra bed," he said, as if he didn't want to impose on me. "I can sleep in your bed, it will be less trouble." I could hardly believe it was actually going to happen. It was a cosmic moment, all because he didn't believe in messing up extra sheets. Another astonishment followed: he didn't want to borrow my extra pajamas. He was actually going to sleep nude. I quickly decided that I would not wear pajamas either. And so we took off our clothes and slept together, hugging and holding each other through the night.

One evening at a party I met a blond young man named Larry, who immediately began touching me as we talked. He said he would like to come see me the next afternoon, still touching me. I told him yes, I was free. The following day I was very excited, unable to concentrate on anything else. I feared that he would not show up, and when it grew late, I became depressed and miserable. Then he arrived. I felt that the polite thing to do was to make some tea. I sat down for some conversation, but he began rubbing me instead of talking. I forgot what I was going to say. Soon I was being led, not unwillingly, to the bedroom.

Another new experience: a person who was eager to have sex with me. When it was over I felt guilty. Shouldn't I show some other kind of interest in him? Wasn't that what he really had visited me for? I tried to show interest in his work. Otherwise, I feared he would think I had only wanted sex. It never occurred to me that *he* had only wanted sex.

Contrasting situations developed with several other people. I would meet someone, perhaps at a party, and then see him a few times for dinner, for an afternoon trip to the beach, or for a quiet time of listening to music. My new friend would be very receptive to spending time together this way. I would feel a warm attraction and want more physical closeness. He would say he did not feel a physical attraction, although he enjoyed knowing me. I would presently say no to the relationship, fearing that I would invest much time in what would turn out to be a merely social friendship, something I had had too much of already in my life. I felt a stigma attached to my insistence on a more physical relationship. I did not give my "no" equal stature with his. It seemed to me that he was taking the high ground, while I was wrongly seeking sex.

It was hard for me openly to declare that what I wanted was sexual friendships. Although the gay world was full of people who simply wanted sex with little or no relationship, I felt ashamed of wanting this. When I said no to a more slowly developing friendship, I acted in a way that felt and no doubt was unreasonable and impatient, but at a deeper level there was a gradual affirmation of my right to think of myself as a sexual being. I did have the right to an irresponsible sexual adolescence, and in a painfully awkward way I was trying to tell myself about that right.

The gay world was always a somewhat strange place to me; I still felt much more myself with college students who were not gay, or when I was by myself in nature. One late winter morning I took a vacation from these difficult encounters and drove down the coast, headed for the state beach at San Gregorio for a day by myself watching the ocean. I spent it at the far southern end of the beach, watching an occasional couple or family walk by, feeling lonely but steady, enjoying the wild cliffs and surf. In the afternoon I walked slowly back. On the way, I glanced up and saw a young man sitting in the sand beneath the cliffs. I turned away quickly, not wanting to be caught looking, but received the distinct impression that he had smiled. Did I dare look again? I walked a few steps and shot a split-second glance. He was looking straight at me and laughing. I walked faster, staring straight ahead as if I had seen nothing.

I glanced again, even faster, the angle now slightly rearward. He was still grinning and getting up to leave. He must be stoned, I told myself, and walked onward. It must be just a coincidence that he was leaving at the same time I was. I was excited. He was very attractive—what a great thing if I could meet him. But of course it was impossible, I told myself. I walked on and he walked on some distance behind me.

Finally we were almost parallel while crossing a stream, and the parking lot was just ahead. I made up my mind to speak to him, no matter how unreceptive he might be. The rejection could be classified as one more scientific experiment, of which my journey as a whole was composed. "It's beautiful here, I hate to leave so soon," I said. "Do you want to smoke a joint?" he asked. "I'm sorry, I don't have any," I replied. "I meant, would you like to smoke one of mine," he said, taking several neatly rolled joints from his pocket. I decided there was nothing to lose, but I pointed to a high bluff overlooking the ocean where we would be less conspicuous. He seemed to find something about me that he liked. And in a few minutes he told me why he thought I was enjoying him. "I am being 'company' for you," he said. I liked the idea of "company."

He was eighteen, a high school dropout, living in Cupertino. He was planning to hitchhike but asked me if I would drive him home instead. At a beautiful place in the hills along the highway, he suggested we pull off onto a small dirt road for a few minutes to look back at the view. He stood close to me, touching me, squeezing my hand. Soon we got back in the car and drove over the hills, and I let him off in front of his house. He said he would like to come see me in San Francisco.

He did come to my apartment a week later. At first we felt very uncomfortable together. We took a walk, but that did not help. "Do you have some dope around?" he questioned me when we got back. We became thoroughly wrecked. There was an old black and white movie on television. It seemed really funny and soon we were comfortably holding hands again. Later in the evening he asked if he could stay over. But I felt that was too much, and drove him to a place from which he could hitchhike home.

My reasons for not encouraging him to stay seemed sensible, although I keenly wanted him to. I had told him I was gay and he had told me he was not. I did not know what was in his mind about the night, or what would happen. If something sexual happened, I would have felt responsible, and I did not want that responsibility. We saw each other every few months after that and the same pattern recurred. I was mystified, but always enjoyed our unexplained friendship.

At a gay party I saw a college student sitting by himself looking withdrawn, and I went over to talk with him. His name was Bruce, and he seemed glad that I showed an interest in him. I gave him my telephone number, not expecting ever to hear from him, but the next afternoon he called. I was thrilled at what seemed the miracle of an intelligent, appealing, young man who actually called *me!* We had dinner, and then he returned to his college, some distance from the city. A few days later a note arrived, saying he would like to visit me the following weekend. It made a great impression on me that it was signed "love" in purple ink. Each day until then my excitement and anticipation mounted. On Friday before his visit I was so filled with anxiety that everything should go well, I was almost sick. I felt like I had the flu. Here was the opportunity to begin a beautiful relationship with someone I really liked—who could be a friend, lover, student, everything—and the weekend might be ruined!

Bruce was due to arrive in the early evening, and I made elaborate preparations. I lit candles to make my apartment romantic and sat around to wait. Hours passed, and there was no sign of him. I knew he was hitchhiking, but could not understand what was keeping him. The candles burned so low that I had to put them all out and return to electric lights.

Around eleven-thirty, after my anxiety had repeatedly driven me out into the street, then back to be sure I could hear the telephone, Bruce finally arrived with a complicated explanation of his delay. But he soon fell totally silent, and there was nothing to do but go to bed. I had carefully thought out the sleeping arrangements, and decided he should sleep in one room and me in another; I had heard many warnings about the dangers of being intimate too soon. When I told him my plan and reason he said, "I'd like to sleep with you, but I do mean just sleep. I'm exhausted." I watched as he took off his clothes and got into my bed, instantly falling fast asleep.

For me it was not so easy. I could not sleep a wink. I was rigid with excitement, strangeness, frustrated desire, in bed with a beautiful long-haired young man. In the morning he showed every sign of sleeping until noon. Unable to bear lying awake next to him any longer, I very quietly got up and stole away to the Mark Hopkins for breakfast, returning to his side in bed at 11 A.M. without his even noticing my absence. I kept hoping something sexual would happen, but when he finally woke up, he said, "Wow, I've really over-slept," and leaped out of bed.

We had a day of shopping, visiting an art gallery, and dinner at a restaurant, during all of which we were barely relating. That night he explained that for him, sleeping with friends was commonplace, and meant no more than being friendly. Since I had had so many expectations, he said he would feel more comfortable spending the second night by himself in the other room.

For the next few days I felt thoroughly depressed, overwhelmed with how hard it all was, and blaming myself for mishandling a situation that I still believed had offered great promise. But at another level I could dimly see that I had not understood him and he had not understood me. It could be very hard to connect with another person.

One day in late spring at a party I was introduced to Adrian, an astrologer, a young man with exotic hand-sewn clothes and a graceful air. The first thing he did was to smile warmly and touch me; there seemed to be an immediate attraction; we saw each other the following day, and the almost mystical feeling of connection was even stronger. Adrian was a student of the occult and the magical, and he accepted the unlikely as perfectly natural. "You are beautiful," he told me, and I was flooded with joy.

At last someone was really drawn to me, and I to him! Nothing else mattered. I lay awake at night dreaming and planning. We would build a life together. And the omens seemed to agree. Adrian was about to move from the house where he had been staying. Olga's horoscope column in the *Chronicle* told me, "Act, Taurus, Act." That was all I needed.

We went to an open hilltop overlooking the ocean and I said, "Come live with me and be my love." I told him we should try living together and that while it might not work out, there was nothing to lose, and he agreed. "I can't believe this is really happening," he said to me, and I told him, "I've wanted this so long." A few days later, with all of his belongings, he moved into my spare room.

From the first moment it was all wrong. Adrian was talented, creative, remarkable. But we were so different. Suddenly he seemed strange, foreign, too exotic. What about all the rest of my life, I asked myself. What about the sides of me that he could not share—Yale, the lawyer, the side that needed to be alone? Was it really possible that Adrian was to be *the* person in my life? Could I possibly share his world? My whole sense of self and security were overwhelmed by fear and a feeling of being trapped.

I tried to ride it out, hoping my misgivings would go away, as we kept to our separate rooms in the apartment.

My whole elaborate system of keeping myself steady broke down, and I felt unstable and unable to function. I saw all the things I admired in Adrian—his courage and independence, his originality, his belief in himself, his remarkable spirit. But I was numb, seeing him through a glass wall. At last the situation became unbearable. Fortunately we found a house which Adrian liked very much and to which he was able to move with help from me. We accepted our mistake.

Adrian is always associated in my mind with magic. He was powerfully connected to the magical world. Nothing more perfectly epitomizes the changes in me than my willingness to accept magic, after a lifetime of being strictly rational. I saw it as a higher reason, indicating the presence of that which exists but is unknown. To recover that belief, the belief in something larger, was another unlooked-for place to which my search had led me.

After the experience with Adrian my Clement Street journey was over. I had no more forward-going energy. I revisited the by-now-familiar places in the city, but it was time for a rest. At Sixth and Clement, nearby my fantasy apartment, I reflected on how much I had seen and learned.

In many ways I felt dissatisfied and confused. My efforts to make contact with another person left me still unfulfilled. I would be returning to Yale as lonely as when I left. I was far from being the confident and serene person I had pictured living near Clement Street. But I did feel more free. I had flooded my life with newness—I felt the winds of change, yet did not know in which direction they would take me.

I came back to Yale to begin the next school year of teaching. Slowly the optimism and freedom of San Francisco disappeared, and once again I was restless, bored, and anxious. I struggled to understand what I had learned in San Francisco. But my mind did not work as capably as it had in that freer setting. I felt clouds of obscurity and confusion which threatened to prevent me from finding any clarity. Mostly I kept to myself at home, working at the table in my kitchen. I did not want anyone to know how needy and desperate, how close to panic I was, a lost person among apparently purposeful students and confident, serious professors.

And yet I knew that I had made the discovery I was searching for. I had caught a glimpse of my true self—my soul. I had seen that it was not dead but a prisoner. And it was my own false knowledge and false conditioning which kept me imprisoned. Because of alienation, my own actions and responses did not obey the needs and desires of my true self. Instead, my actions and responses oppressed and betrayed my soul. Alienation had severed the connection between my soul and my behavior in the external world.

It never occurred to me to question the authenticity of my own actions. I could not imagine that they betrayed my true self. I felt so honest, so sincere, so guided by principle, so idealistic. I always believed that what I was doing was "right." If I failed to find love, I blamed the world or I blamed my "situation." I was blind to the fact that nurture was there all the time, in me and in others, and that my own misguided responses and mistaken actions imprisoned me.

The ideals and yearnings which my soul felt were all true enough. But when I looked at the external world I was totally deceived as to what could fill those needs, like a person who yearns for self-respect and believes an expensive automobile will provide this. Alienation substitutes false objects for those which might truly serve our souls. At the same time, it steers us away from what might actually satisfy our desires.

I thought back to the moment when I had broken through the boundary of sexuality. For my whole life I had been totally starved of sex. All of those years were spent in a kind of insanity of isolation, for no one ever touched me and I touched no one. I was a stricken island, cut off from my fellow beings. I could not imagine calling out for help.

It was my conditioning that led me to believe that a man could not ask anyone for help with his fears concerning sex—that a man had to seem competent and self-assured even when he was not—that in the area of sex, ignorance and fear were somehow inadmissible and would make people think less of him. My role as a professor, author, or intellectual implied that I was competent to meet my needs and would not have to seek help from people in any area of life.

My conditioning also made me prejudiced against homosexuality, even though it was a major element of my own nature. Without ever really thinking about it, sex between men seemed hideous and repulsive, and desiring sex with a man seemed to reveal a morally diseased impulse. I thought that to be homosexual meant being weak, campy, a deviant. I could not imagine a calm, strong, decisive homosexual man. I felt that no person would ever have any reason to desire a relationship with someone of his or her own sex—that homosexuals were people who couldn't find the real thing.

I had not learned to distinguish fears and prejudices—in me or in those to whom I tried to relate—from the positive feelings that might exist but for such barriers. Since I was so miserable and alone, since my struggles toward other people never succeeded, it must be because I was totally undesirable, rather than because they had fears or I myself had fears.

My mind had been filled with unquestioned false assumptions about myself and about reality, all of which I was certain I "knew." Conditioning thrives on its ability to remain undetected. If the barriers were invisible, then there was left the apparent reality that I, though filled with a yearning for closeness, could never find anyone. I blamed myself for lack of connection.

Another way I had been kept in ignorance about sex was the artificial separation of elements that should have been together in my mind. There were secret fantasy thoughts about men, but I did not connect these to genital sexual contact. There was something called the homosexual world, but I connected it to dark, bizarre, evil activities, not to love, closeness, or friendship. And there were my blocked feelings concerning women. I did not imagine that sexual feelings toward women could be similar to my suppressed fantasies about men. The wholeness and integration of all these disparate elements was at the center of the missing truth.

Even the brief and limited experience with the models showed me that I was missing so much: whispering, laughing, teasing, tickling, cuddling, feeling warm and protected. These were things I had desperately yearned for all my life, and finally with the models I was able to experience them. So many days and nights of emptiness had been spent starving for these undeciphered needs.

I had come to believe that I was a person with an exceptionally low degree of sensuality and sexual ease—a stiff, tense, anxious, inhibited person. Sex seemed no more my métier than surfing. My own responses did not count. The way I felt when I became aroused did not count as sex. My attraction to men did not count as love. My desire to snuggle with people was not what "mature" people wanted. Sex that "counted," I believed, was a smooth and confident performance of sexual intercourse with a woman—the woman passive, the man cool and controlling.

My eyes had been opened to the fact that there were many other ways to be sexual—with a greater equality of roles, without performance and control, with emotion instead of coolness. Sex could be playful or tender, intimate rather than athletic.

My sexual predicament showed how the individual alienation of my formative years and the alienation represented by social attitudes combined to build a wall against sex of any kind. My childhood left me with a general fear of intimacy and a specific fear of intimacy with women. Society added negative feelings about closeness to men. The result was to cut me off from a form of nurture every human being needs.

I had passed the age of forty without being able to give or receive sexual love with any man or woman, and yet all of this time my soul yearned for sexual love. But I did not know how to provide for my own needs in the most elementary way. In the deepest sense I—my soul—did not know what "I"—my external self—was doing. And so, though I felt I had a loving soul, in actuality I remained an unloving person, a molecule at odds with my fellow beings and the universe, a molecule of anarchy and disconnection, needy and starving.

I saw my own personal history from a new perspective. In Washington alienation held sway over me, and I made almost no successful efforts to combat it. The new consciousness era of the late sixties showed me that I could be different, but I did not know how to change on my own. And in the early seventies I was swept back into yet deeper alienation.

The form of liberation I finally discovered in San Francisco consisted of radically questioning the authenticity of my own actions and responses, to see if they actually did serve the commands of my true self. I permitted myself new choices—ones I had never before dared. By trial and error, I discovered how better to serve my own needs. Once I had discovered one self-deception, others became apparent. In area after area I had questioned the validity of what I knew about myself. I questioned my fears and my negative feelings about relationships. I questioned the pessimistic assumption that I could never experience closeness. I allowed myself to discover feelings I did not think I had. I trusted the deepest voices within me.

I could be happier, have more energy, know myself better, be more responsible for myself, be more loving and more free. I could continue to change in the same direction as people had changed during the late sixties. Like the sixties people, my changes were at the level of basic values. But while people in the sixties were swept along by an atmosphere that encouraged change, I had found a way to make similar changes on my own, despite the pessimistic trend in the culture of the 1970's. The power to make changes lies within each individual and is not dependent on the times.

Change was not brought about by awareness alone, I had found. An essential condition of change was learning how to better satisfy one's own needs. Change was supported by better psychic and emotional nutrition, better nurture. Thus change was not mystical or unexplainable, but a perfectly straightforward process, just as a plant grows when its needs are met. Change was possible because I had been severely and artificially limited by alienation, and therefore I had hidden, untapped powers within me.

I saw that many forms of personal exploration, therapy and experimentation could help people to accomplish what I had started to accomplish, provided that they thereby learned to question the authenticity of their own actions and responses. That was the key—to learn the ways in which one betrayed and oppressed oneself. The whole personal growth movement could be seen as part of a great battle against alienation, and my own efforts were one individual part of this battle.

In the perspective of this battle, I saw that my sexual explorations had been concerned less with sex than with a yearning for connection. My real need was to end my isolation, to share the dailiness of life, to share my work and thoughts, to feel a part of something larger than myself. If sex was an opening to intimacy, intimacy might be a gateway to this larger sharing. I did not yet know what fears or ignorance held me back from being part of a couple relationship, or a family, or a community. But I began to feel that if I found these connections, sex would become less important, certainly less desperate—merely one form of sharing, although an especially beautiful experience to me. Sex alone—alienated sex—I already recognized to be another illusion or deception, another empty goal. But because the need for sex could still be heard within me, even when the inner voices crying for other forms of connection and sharing had become inaudible, sex had guided me to the more deeply hidden needs. It was the beginning of my healing, my first reconnection to myself, the first drifting log that told of land ahead.

Surely my greatest unhappiness all through my life had come from lack of connection. Recognizing this, I could look around me and see the world in new terms. For what I had been missing, others must be missing too. I was not alone. In others, the sexual connection might exist, but some other connection—to the imagination, to creativity, to the power of self-belief—might be missing. Loss of connection could be recognized as the ailment of the nation as a whole.

Without connection there can be force but not power. Power is not force but the ability to influence other people and the environment through the surge of your own ability to nurture and create. Without connection there is a profound loss of knowledge. It is difficult to understand or sympathize with or remain conscious of that with which we do not connect. Our long-time "ignorance" of environment and our national government's inability to comprehend Asia are illustrations of such lack of knowledge. Happiness, value and meaning are the consequences of connection and are lost by lack of connection.

To substitute for connections that are lost, we have connections that are contrived. Think of an office, a factory, a crowded subway train, or a traffic jam as forced connection. It may have a purpose, as a factory or corporate office does. But if pressure of any kind is necessary to maintain the connection, we pay a heavy price. For then we have to rely on punishment and pressure to carry out social policy.

One of the characteristics of an alienated government

is a pervasive detachment from people, culture, and society, all of which it increasingly deals with by ignorance, pretense, or force. There are degrees of detachment and different kinds of detachment, but detachment is the common denominator. A senator who warned about the cruelties of the war in Vietnam was less detached than a President who continued the war. But if that senator still believed in a war on crime, it would reveal ignorance and detachment in another area. The President who refuses amnesty to those who would not aid in the war against Vietnam shows lack of connection. The Vietnam war itself was a colossal lack of connection.

At last I had a point of view from which I could understand what was happening to society. I saw that all of my efforts to understand government, law, and the steady deterioration of our values had failed to take account of the fact that people are adversely affected by conditioning and cut off from nurture whether they are aware of it or not. As people become more unable to connect, their institutions and systems become unable to function.

For half my life, as a student and teacher of government, law, and the American system, I had been unable to see the reason for the events, trends, and crises I studied. Nor had I seen the pattern they formed. I had been looking in the wrong direction. I had my eyes fixed on the system, where changes were reflected but not caused. I wrote warnings about what I saw, but not about the true source of what I saw. Now I turned to the changes taking place in people, and I felt that there was a convincing reason for what was happening to our world. *A starving people, with diminishing self-knowledge, would make any system fail.* They would not know what they were doing, and our leaders and institutions would not know what they were doing. They would no longer know how to act in the best interests of human beings, as individuals or as a society.

I finally recognized that people were the great unseen, unmeasured variable in society. People could change and be changed, either healthfully through the recognition by themselves and by others of their inherent worth and dignity, or by being starved and diminished from a lack of nurture. But this immensely important fact was virtually ignored by those who sought to understand or to govern our society. It was omitted from history, science, sociology, law. It was assumed that people remained the same while the formal structure of society grew and changed. But that assumption takes no note of conditioning. Alienation and conditioning can modify "human nature." People could vary; variations in people formed a part of our history, and part of the influence on our way of life. But we did not recognize this, had no monitors to see if it were true, and seemed to consider such modification a scientific and intellectual impossibility.

I could see in every part of society the human element disappearing. Richness of design had vanished from buildings, personal character was lost in chain businesses, transactions with professionals became more anonymous. The Supreme Court was steadily destroying the privilege against self-incrimination. In Congress, impersonal corporate interests were represented far more heavily than the feelings of the average citizen. Authenticity was lacking in a President's speeches filled with manufactured phrases. The individual participant in sports could get less nurture in the form of self-expression and closeness to others. The sports fan could get less nurture from Astroturf and contract negotiations among sports figures. The automobile driver on a freeway could get less nurture from the countryside than the more leisurely motorist on the two-lane roads of thirty years ago. In terms of real needs of individuals, the country was becoming a place of starvation. No wonder I felt worse and worse at Yale and in New Haven; I *was* worse, and my bad feelings reflected the spreading alienation.

All of this set the stage for the catastrophe of the seventies: a rapidly worsening collapse of human hopes. There was a spiritual desolation. The country was depleted of energy, bravery, and power to change. America, once our sweet land of liberty, had become a harsh and alien desert where we were forced to struggle for survival.

The fabric of life was ripped apart. Cities were wasted by crime, mental unbalance, physical rot, decline of public spirit and service, and a desperate sense that no one knew what was happening. Politics and government were the province of lies, corruption, special interests, and lawless misuse of power. The nation seemed to be going backwards, returning to policies and leaders already proven to be failures. While often pouring energy into useless pursuits and false values, our real selves were increasingly neglected. Inevitably we became more dependent and needy, easily prey to any oversimple answer. Spreading addiction of every kind—to drugs, alcohol, material comforts, unhealthy relationships—gave evidence of our inner wasting. Our feelings were no longer heard, and therefore could no longer guide us to survival. As a result, although we could see the deterioration around us, and although we kept on pretending that we were still in control, within ourselves we knew despair.

But now this helplessness could end. We could regain power and reassert responsibility for our country. We could do so because *we* were the cause of what was happening, of all that was happening. We could accept this fact about ourselves if we could see our conditioning as alien and not as our authentic selves, and that we had power to recognize and fight our conditioning, and to begin the process of fundamental change.

If I was starving, I must take responsibility for that fact. No matter that I had been deceived, conditioned, alienated, kept ignorant of my needs. If I wanted to be free, I must accept responsibility for my own nurture. If I could not take care of myself, I forfeited my freedom. No amount of blame of others or justifications or excuses could change my responsibility to myself. In this knowledge lay my road to freedom.

A basic error of our time was the public denial of the disastrous state of our lives and our own society. We did not admit to each other how bad we felt, how bad the system made us feel. We thought it looked stronger for us to act as if we were feeling fine. When the Supreme Court lost dignity through the appointment of less reverent men, we did not allow ourselves to cry out at the loss. When redwood forests were being destroyed, we repressed our feelings, and so the loss was "invisible." When we began to let ourselves feel the pain of that natural loss, the ecology movement was born, starting a small shift in the opposite direction. But the ecology of our society as a whole was continuing to be wrecked, and we were still pretending otherwise. In consequence, we did not register the true extent to which the existing system affronted our souls.

By denying our losses, we were led to deny responsibility for having made choices that brought us to the point of social and individual disintegration. Instead we claimed that we were powerless as individuals and blamed something called The System or "human nature." We could conclude that no power existed anywhere to make a new choice. Thereby we would forfeit faith in our ability to enact change. By pointing a finger elsewhere, by denying that we as individuals could choose the values that we as a people might collectively choose, we manifested this failure to take responsibility.

But if we could see that our world is exactly what we have chosen, the precise expression of how much and how little we have taken responsibility for ourselves, then the possibility of another choice returns. We can say: *This is the world I have chosen.* The acceptance of responsibility that is truly ours is not, as it might imply, a burden to be avoided at all costs, but the definitive liberation from the tyrannies of alienation, resignation, and despair.

In a society where the people's actions do not correspond with their own inner values or desires, they send inappropriate instructions to their government and the government bases its decisions on a mistaken series of assumptions about the people. This whole dark comedy of misinformation and mistaken actions is presided over by public officials who are usually chosen from the most alienated of all—the individuals whose ambition for power and status is the dominating element in their lives. Such leaders readily believe the alienated instructions they receive and add their own alienation as they turn their assumptions into political decisions. Where alienation holds sway, the collective power of the people is turned back against them as a gigantic mechanism of oppression.

I finally saw alienation as a fundamental form of tyranny, comparable to fascism and totalitarianism. It creates a social system and government which both denies us access to our needs and deceives us into putting our labor into that which serves only the state and does us only harm. It is a society in which officially sanctioned injury to the individual enforces a tormented servitude to material goods and empty institutional structures. It denies fundamental human rights—autonomy, freedom of choice, the right not to be arbitrarily hurt, the right not to be unjustly deprived of one's happiness. It denies the people power to take care of their own lives.

An alienated society is no less a political tyranny because the oppression is found within each individual, rather than coming from a single source such as an army or a dictator. For our self-oppression is no more our free choice than the decrees of a dictator. Self-oppression is merely a more advanced form of tyranny than totalitarianism. Armies and police are not needed to enforce most of the state's commands, but only to punish unruly selves for expressing their suffering through crime, addiction, and civil unrest.

An alienated society is not the land of the free. There is no freedom for a people with falsely conditioned minds. Choices are made for them, and their minds are closed to other choices. They march in formation at the bidding of a force outside themselves. Their independence has been cut off at its roots. They carry the American flag, but they no longer know the American spirit. They do not possess the power of self-reliance, for they cannot trust themselves. They are no longer free citizens, for they deny their own responsibility by not heeding the commands of their true selves, by no longer knowing and keeping faith with their own souls. They can no longer worship, for they are in ignorance of the god within.

Sitting at my table late at night, with the single overhead light coming down and making an island in the darkness, I pictured my small apartment in New Haven as an ever-narrowing, ever more barren and oppressive cell, pressed on by the barriers of numbness, fear, and disappearing knowledge. And outside the barriers, I now knew, was a whole green world that contained freedom and nurture, if I could only get there.

Could I enter that new world, beyond the invisible barriers of conditioning? Could I hold on to it, learn the secrets of how to live permanently in the green places? Dared I leave my cell, which had provided a narrow security for so long? Were there other people out there? Could I become a new person in the world?

The single light was all that offered safety from that which surrounded and pressed in on my small apartment and me, the only illumination against the encroaching darkness.

The
Road

Five

I took my first steps on the road entirely alone. When I left my New Haven apartment in the morning for the campus, I allowed pain to show in my face. In class, I was not so ready to please students, and sometimes the attendance would drop off. When students visited my home, I told them I was gay, which quickly made them become more distant. I avoided social events that could have drawn me out of my unhappiness but offered nothing more lasting. I developed more ways to care for, and be compassionate toward myself. What I achieved was greater honesty and a more realistic view of my situation.

I found that Yale increasingly denied any reality other than its own. With all the upheavals in law—from Watergate to the steady decay of institutions like prisons and public welfare—the law school continued on its way with an unnerving complacency. At the college level, intense focusing on grades by both faculty and students seemed to disregard the instability outside. The world of Washington, D.C., and the young lawyer had engulfed the one-time sanctuary of Yale.

I had continued at Yale despite the increasing attractiveness of San Francisco because I still believed that by seeking a combination of personal and institutional change I would be active in building a better world. But I found that without support I was unable to maintain my new self for more than a few days, even after it was strengthened by occasional visits to San Francisco. It appeared that to be free of alienation, no matter how determined I was, I must have an outside support system or else be swept along by the current. Without support by people, natural beauty, an attractive city, and intellectual progress, I was too depressed to be a positive force for change, either internally or externally.

When you are comfortably established in a certain reality, and that reality becomes less hospitable toward you, what can you do? If you stay and allow the real nurture of your life to shrink while no one around you acknowledges this fact, so that all are diminished at an even rate, like people going down in an elevator together while seeming to be standing still—then imperceptibly you too will diminish so that your powers will lessen, and your energy and ability to love will shrivel, your openness to nature will close, your generosity will wither, your trust will grow shaky. And you will become less able to love yourself, to be yourself, to be with yourself; you will lose the company of yourself. This was my fate if I remained; that is the truth I finally had to face.

I needed to learn exactly how I had been made to believe in my unhappy fate. I had to realize that my fate was not the result of being permanently ignorant and deprived of power but merely something I had learned. I had built myself into a safe but sterile fortress because I did not think I could safely navigate in the open world. I dared not share my feelings of inadequacy, and so I went through many years without truly being able to share my feelings with anyone. I was locked up in a lonely tower of silence, with a view out toward all the others whom I could never touch.

I thought to myself: We rarely acknowledge how much we despise ourselves for our failings, for our betrayal of the possibilities within us for honesty, for love, for greatness. We do not talk about this self-hatred because we actually believe it is our duty to become what we are not—and to the degree that we succeed, we may also succeed in life, so that society rewards us for the degree of alienation we achieve. We receive high school diplomas and college degrees and master's degrees and doctorates of philosophy in self-violation and self-betrayal.

Our self-hatred is everywhere in our actions and talk if we can but see it. We lie, we betray, we evade, we pretend, we hide, we cover our discontent, we smother our true beliefs. We live in ways in which we do not believe, and pretend not to want the things that we most need and desire. We all join the conspiracy and oppress one another. We hide our pain and our wounds, and therefore compel others to hide theirs. All of us are afraid, but we fear each other instead of the system that victimizes us.

We hide our inadequacies and submit silently to our fate because we take the blame for our inadequacy on ourselves. This self-hatred pervades our society today, from top to bottom, destroying the solidarity that might exist between people who are entitled to a better fate. I feel we must cry out in anger and pain at our supposed inadequacies, failures, inferiority. We must tell ourselves that it is all an unjust lie.

We need to see how our capacity for happiness and genius has been lost and that we have been trained from birth to accept a lesser fate. Then we can rebel and declare that we will change our fate. We can declare, as the first principle of human rights in our day, that the alienation we have all learned can be unlearned, and that it is for the good of all that we unlearn it. We can love ourselves, and only then will we begin to grow into our true greatness.

During the spring of 1974 I finally made up my mind to resign my position at Yale. The reasons for leaving had been obvious to me for a long time. The students, both in the college and in the law school, were increasingly the prisoners of the kind of alienation that had separated me from my true self in Washington, D.C. It became harder and harder to teach them or be friends with them, and my own changes only increased the distance. My enjoyment of the full-time teacher's role lessened, so that I dreaded the days when classes met, and looked forward only to my writing. There simply were no more supports for my life in New Haven. I was leaving Yale, but in a very deep sense, Yale had already left me. It was no longer the place I had enthusiastically come to fourteen years earlier. In 1960 the ideal dominating Yale was optimistic intellectual searching. By 1974 I felt survival and careerism dominated all but the most idealistic handful of people. Locked college gates and barred windows of campus buildings made Yale a fortress against the surrounding inner city. If I stayed I would die by inches and by degrees of chattering cold. If I left now, while I still had enough self-trust to do so, maybe I could find something waiting for me.

Without realizing it, I had grown deeply dependent on Yale. Even after all of the problems there had become clear, I still had to face the tremendous insecurity of leaving the major reality of my life. Could I possibly find a meaningful working life away from a large institution? Would I be able to meet new people on my own? Was I independent enough to survive without a defined world in which I had a place? Could I feel that my work was joined to the work of others? I had to break a fourteen-year dependency, one that everyone who remained at Yale warned me against breaking, for they all seemed to feel that Yale was the only reality in which people like me could survive and find security with meaning. To leave such a familiar world I had to believe that I could create a new one. I had to imagine that something out there could fill the void I would experience from this departure. But if I could honestly make myself see that the emptiness was there already, that the old forms of what I loved were hollow, and if I knew that there was more in me than I had shown, I could then take a chance—not on the outside world alone, but on the buried and unexpressed parts of myself. I said to myself: I can be greater, I can be more. I might be totally cynical in public all day long and run down myself and the entire human race, but before the temple of myself, lies and self-deception are swept away into silence. And in that pure moment, I found enough self-love to say *yes,* I am out of the prison bars, the gates, the walls, and away and free. I set forth.

I arrived in San Francisco in May, 1974. My foot, which had been causing me to limp all during the spring, was so swollen and painful that I went straight from the airport to the doctor. It turned out to be a ruptured Achilles tendon, and the doctor wanted to operate immediately. That night was spent in the hospital, with an operation coming the next morning.

The surgery on my heel was in some mysterious way a beginning. I felt this might be the case, but I couldn't foresee how. For a week I lay in the hospital room with my leg in a cast up on two pillows, wondering what was coming, dozing away the hours, watching the soap operas or talking on the phone. When I finally got back to my San Francisco home, writing and convalescing became my major activities.

The cast came off in August, but my physical ordeal was not over—it had just begun. The surgical wound reopened, which sometimes happens after Achilles tendon operations despite the best of care, and I found myself with a deep, wide hole in my leg which would take many more months to heal. I felt as though I had been visited by the plagues of Egypt: my pain and anxiety increased; infections in the wound and a fungus infection on my foot made walking more than a few steps difficult; there was an allergic reaction on my hands, so that tenderness and itching made writing a struggle; and I had problems with my stiff neck, bad back, and gout. My whole body was crying out that it had been neglected. The summer and fall passed and the weekly visits to the doctor continued.

In early January, the open wound in my heel became infected, and by the next day I was back in the hospital more ill than I had ever been before, with a 105° fever, a massive headache, chills, and dizziness. I had streptococcus septicemia—a dangerous and once fatal blood poisoning. I lay in my hospital bed with a rubber intravenous device attached to my arm, my leg swollen up and wrapped in wet dressings, and doctors and nurses coming and going. I was exhausted but not sleeping—devastated by a staggering blow.

I was plunged into aloneness—no one could share this overwhelming experience. No one could really share the feelings I had—the helplessness, the invasion, the paranoia, and the meaninglessness. I stared out the hospital window in the direction of the ocean and the west—angry, threatened, miserable, and determined to make some meaning from it all.

I reached back for one of the oldest and deepest parts of myself—the survivor. I had survived so much pain, disappointment, and sadness in my life, and I could cope with this ordeal too. The survivor came straight out of my childhood, when I had also felt hemmed in by capricious forces over which I had no control. Every instinct drove me toward order, discipline, and control of whatever small territory (my bureau, closet, or bed) constituted my domain.

Now I found that I was strong enough not merely to endure all of this hardship, but to prosper, and thus put more and more energy into my writing. It feels immensely good to know that you are dealing head-on with everything that comes your way. If you can't safely descend the front steps on crutches without help, go down on your rear end. If you need both hands for crutches, carry pages of the book across the room with your teeth. If you cannot sit up, write lying down. If there are problems with friends, with the apartment, with finances—deal with them, one by one. Running away makes you feel inadequate, and dealing with everything gives you a feeling of strength.

I put an end to making a point-by-point comparison of my life to anyone else's, as I had so painfully done at Yale. Instead, I focused on my own life, and that was as far as I let my thoughts go. More than ever before, I became my own parent, taking better care of myself, nurturing myself with kindness, avoiding all expectations and pressure, and allowing myself the necessary time and space to recover from the sadness, shock, and pain.

As time went on, my body's struggle to heal itself became a metaphor for a deeper process within—one in which my inner self cried out that it too had been neglected and had wounds that could at last be healed. I could feel myself becoming whole again. Nothing had been lost or cut off beyond a possibility of reconnection. I had no reason for cynicism, bitterness, or blame. Nothing had been taken, just misplaced. All of me is still here, I realized; I can be true to the whole person that I am.

I have the strength of the Old Ones. I have always lived the Hard Way. The Hard Way is at the top of your register from crisis to crisis, from tragedy to tragedy, from heroic effort to heroic effort, from glee to glee, from sorrow to sorrow. The Old Ones are like ancient gnarled Victorian houses standing between modern stucco homes. The Old Ones are ill-suited to today's conditions, like my white-haired and regal great-grandmother from Alsace-Lorraine, who at eighty-seven invariably stood in the parlor if the radio played the "Marseillaise."

For me there need be no forgetting or throwing away. Being whole, I can remember all of myself, the undiminished intensity of my happiness and my pain. I can remember my own dreams and my country's dreams. I can remember in all its fullness the truth of all the love I have felt, and therefore dare to love again.

I felt a new love for my parents. When I stopped holding my parents responsible for my fate, I could begin to see them as old friends. I thought of my parents in the same dimension that I used for thinking of young people. I thought of their hopes, their tenderness and vulnerability, their courage in the face of the long unknown road ahead with all its hardships and promise. Was there ever a more magical time than the late twenties and early thirties in New York City—the time of Art Deco dreams? The miracle of radio. Movies—not as we see them now but fresh and wonderful as they were then. Swing and jazz, new dances. Stunning modern clothes for women and for men. Gleaming apartment houses and restaurants with mirrors and metal and style and chic. A new mood of freedom, sophistication, and optimism. The great sleek ocean liners that could carry one with glamour and romance to Europe. The soaring, shining skyscrapers like monuments to a new human dream. I saw my parents young and beautiful in that world.

My new fate in San Francisco first appeared to me in the form of Katherine, a young woman who lived in the outer Richmond District. Kathy, who was medium tall with soft brown hair, had a warmth and openness that even strangers responded to. She was a friend of one of the people helping me through my convalescence. She began stopping by to see me on her way home from work. She brought cookies and made her favorite tea (a blend of rosehips and lemon grass), and soon we became good friends. Kathy had led a hippie lifestyle in the late sixties and she still believed in the truth of those days. I told her that I was gay, and I secretly felt excited at the idea of a relationship with a woman. When we grew warmer and more affectionate, I did not find myself drawing back, but was grateful and happy.

While I felt lost because I had experienced so little in

the way of closeness to other people, Katherine was lost in a different way; she had had many relationships but felt trapped and unfulfilled in her work. She wanted to be an artist, but continued to work at the Bank of America downtown, not confident enough to break away and devote her energy to becoming a creative person. We decided that we could encourage and sustain each other.

Kathy was wise, calm, funny, and gentle with me. She paid me a lot of attention, pointing out ways in which I could change, being lovingly critical of my ingrained eccentricities. I asked her to help me learn about closeness, about loving, and how to acquire the ease with relationships that she had. And I offered to help her believe in herself, learn how to be more motivated and disciplined, and begin doing work that she really wanted to do. She brought her sketches and often worked on them while I relaxed.

Gradually we began to discover that we were becoming important to each other, and we tried to make our somewhat unusual relationship work. We agreed to be honest with each other, reporting on what we were thinking and feeling. And since our relationship was a difficult one, with a great difference in age, with major sexual barriers, and with many other differences in background and experience, we agreed to work hard at the relationship, to treat it as an experiment from which there was much to be learned.

As I grew more mobile, we began to do things that were fun. We had lunch at a Vietnamese restaurant on one of the avenues near the ocean. We went to a large party for a glossy, hip magazine where we knew hardly anyone, and that drew us even closer. We went to a bar in Sausalito where we could look across the Bay at the lights of the city.

We ate piroshki and borscht at a Russian bakery. While I sat in her 1964 Valiant with my crutches, Kathy stood in line for hot fudge sundaes at an ice cream parlor in Noe Valley. We began to see more deeply into each other and found kinship. We could be funny in different ways. On Balboa Street Kathy picked a bunch of daisies from somebody's front lawn while I explained to an imaginary policeman that I was not with this lady.

Kathy began to change my appearance, which had received little attention since my days as a young lawyer. To replace my worn-out button-down shirts we shopped for embroidered ones that I would never have chosen myself. She took me to a men's and women's hair salon in Berkeley where the woman who cut my hair gave me permission to stop combing it down, and ruffle it so that it would be more curly.

At some point I might have begun to withdraw had Kathy not been endowed with a marvelous sense of balance. She never once leaned my way at the wrong time. Instead, we were allies in giving each other freedom: our commitment was to help each other to grow and change and become happier. And so for the first time since childhood the closest and most important person in my life was a woman, and I felt transformed. I was proud to be with her, felt less self-conscious, and I looked at the world with more gratitude.

Katherine was the first person who desired and pursued me purely for myself. She sought me out for things that I had never valued before—my smile, my unkempt hair, my eyes, my figure sitting on a bench near the Marina Green, absorbed in my writing. She looked up to me, and perceived beauty and magic in me as if I was sexy, as if I could be a source of joy. When I appeared, she could be surprised into a smile. When she was sad or upset or angry —even at me—I could rock her, tease her, hug her into smiling, or just look into her eyes and make her smile. And so she helped me find immense powers within myself. I discovered the liberation of unconditional love.

Every now and then, we did something glamorous. I became the irresistible leading man taking a shy but thrilled young woman out to dinner at night by the waterside, or walking on the beach in the fog. I was the man for whom she cooked special candlelight dinners. When we walked, she hooked her arm in mine as if I were Cary Grant.

We shared the special language of two people who seemed to be seeing the world afresh through each other's eyes—sailing along the Great Highway, or kissing good-night under the magnolia tree in her front yard. For the first time I felt like the image of my father as he seemed to the admiring eyes of a boy, with his wit, his good looks, and his style. Yes, I was smitten—more than smitten, captivated.

How happy she made me. How many places within me, cold since childhood, were warmed back to life by her soft touch. Never in my life had I been able to share so much with one person, never had I been able to share so much of my own world.

As Kathy grew more attracted to me, she quite naturally and easily suggested that we could have sex. For me, this was a huge barrier, a great issue. I would remind her that I was gay, but the truth was that I wanted this to happen at least as much as she did, but felt afraid. All those years of self-doubt had built a fortress around me. But I saw my chance to fulfill a deeply buried longing.

And so I worked on turning around the great rusty

switches in me that had been in the off position for so long. Much of the work I did in my own head, struggling with the faulty conditioning that had imprisoned me. I saw that my responses were "wrong," for they kept me distant from something good while continuing to lead me toward other people who were immediately attractive to me, but who ultimately might have little to offer. Logic and reason demanded that my responses to Kathy change. They should no longer reflect whatever bad feelings I had from the past concerning women. They should no longer be tied to prejudices that I could not justify. My principles demanded that I be able to be close to anyone—women included—and my responses should no longer defy my principles. I should be able to return feelings that another person was able to give me. Above all, I should be free to love with my body a person I already loved with my mind and my soul. And so I instructed my feelings to change, to make the new connection between my knowledge and my feelings.

Because I was a gay man, I had a most important kind of permission which proved vital. From the earliest days of our friendship there were no sexual expectations. I could touch Kathy without it being considered "sexual," and she could touch me in the same way. We could snuggle close together for a long time with no pressure on me to go farther in the direction of sex. As a supposedly heterosexual man in Washington, D.C., I never felt this kind of freedom. I could make progress at last, because there was no pressure; I could always stop, always be satisfied with the feelings I had. And without expectations, the barriers could begin to fall. I saw myself as a tall, gawky boy of thirteen. At that age I could afford to be awkward, inexperienced, and in need of help. Kathy became an "older woman" for me, and I felt safe in being vulnerable to her in this way. And so my conditioning began to lose its grip. My feelings flowed into the new channels.

One Saturday morning with nothing planned for the entire weekend, we took off our clothes, got in bed together and stayed there until my fears were calmed and we started to warm up to each other, and finally I had sexual intercourse with a woman for the first time. I was filled with joy.

By means of the new channel of communication opened by sexual intercourse, I experienced a flow between two people as never before. I always imagined that such feelings were possible, but they had always eluded me. Now, because I was compelled to go slowly in all sexual motions, slowness itself was revealed as the channel to deeper and deeper feeling.

As time went on, through many painful difficulties as well as happy moments, we kept on loving each other but gave each other more space in which to grow. Neither of us was ready for a total emotional commitment. If we had tried to remain a self-contained couple we would have held each other back. Kathy needed more time to concentrate on her art. I needed to save a large part of myself for writing. I had never had any satisfying gay relationships and I wanted to keep searching in this direction, for I continued to feel that I needed closeness to men as well. Katherine supported this goal of mine and remained an essential part of my life.

Kathy was one of a group of friends in San Francisco who all knew each other and who were dedicated to personal growth. We gave each other a lot of support and reinforcement for our individual efforts to change. From this group of people I gradually felt a sense of safety, comfort, and security—a sense of community. Among my friends, it was easy to talk about one's feelings, easy to be affectionate, easy to share other people's feelings. Occupations varied widely, although it was everyone's goal to do something that she or he sincerely believed in. There was no imposed structure to this group. But there was the sense that people were available to each other, while at the same time each person's goal was autonomy. All of us desired some measure of family feeling and found it in varying degrees with one another.

To me the city became a network of spaces made meaningful and available because of the presence of friends or the location of shared activities. Two or three homes of friends were in the Clement Street neighborhood, so that the area of my fantasy became a warm reality. In the Marina, two friends managed a nursery and plant store, a calm, beautiful, and mystical oasis in the busy shopping area. Other friends made North Beach a more personal neighborhood. Several of us shared the enjoyment of some favorite beaches along the north side of the city facing the Bay, as well as a special affinity for Sundays in Golden Gate Park. As each new place became meaningful, another light would turn on in my map of the city, a friendly beacon in the evening.

Kathy was not the only good consequence of my being on crutches after the hospital. I enlisted the help of half a dozen people who took turns looking after me. Some were former students of mine from Yale, some were sent by San Francisco acquaintances. Gradually several became friends and a regular part of my life.

Steven was in his early twenties, tall and fair, with

glasses and a relaxed, warm smile. He came from a conservative family in the Pacific Northwest. He had grown up with junk food, ball games, church on Sundays, sweatshirts, rebellion against straitlaced school authorities, many casual friends, much time alone in the out-of-doors. He carried a sturdiness with him, a reserve, a hidden dash of rowdiness, a yet deeper dimension of calm. He studied psychology at college, but had become disillusioned with the possibilities of a formal career, feeling that as an institutional psychologist he would be more bureaucratic than creative. Recently he had been marking time in an unrewarding office job. As a teenager in the late sixties he had been swept into the fun and higher awareness of that period, and he was still a strong believer in the late sixties vision. He had long hair and brightly colored T-shirts, was a student of rock music, and was a lover of the shore and salt water. He had done some writing of his own, but so far he had little self-confidence in his own potential.

Steven started out by literally being my arms and legs. On the days when he came, he made breakfast and carried in coffee from the kitchen, for on crutches I could not even carry a coffee cup. Then we would sit opposite each other across the oak table where I wrote. Very gradually his presence there began to change me.

After many years I had grown used to never sharing most of my working life with anyone—not my thought, not my daily routines. In fact, I did not feel it was possible to carry on these central functions of my life in another person's presence; I believed that any person would prevent me from working, disturb my thoughts, interfere with my efficiency in daily life.

Now another person was present during the most crucial parts of my day. At first I was very tense. But Steven took it easy, did not disturb my thoughts, and slipped into his own thoughts or read a book. He could sit opposite me, and still I felt free to keep on working, because Steven was so self-contained. If I talked, he stopped and listened. Gradually I found myself talking to him more and more.

When Steven arrived at nine he brought the newspaper. We would talk about the news and then I would tell him my own "news"—my thoughts and feelings. Then I would go to work, but when I felt stymied by a difficult idea I could turn to Steven and he would listen as I explained the problem. At first he simply listened, but after a while he began to help me with the problems. He could give me clarity and perspective. At Yale I had the classroom, and individual students and faculty members, as forums for my ideas, and Steven became all of these people in one.

Steven began adding his own beliefs and his own way of seeing to our work. Energy began to flow between us. I would start by telling Steven the problem I was working on, and he would ask for clarification. I learned to respect his questions for they pointed straight at the obscurities of my thinking. I would try to expand and clarify. If I went too speedily and began to stumble, Steven would slow me down. If I was overcomplicated, Steven would restate the idea with a refreshing simplicity, or he might offer ideas of his own. I discovered that he could add breadth to my thoughts and knowledge. In time we found ourselves to be co-workers, and the same projects became a channel for two persons' energy, creativity, and commitment. And something happened that would have been impossible in Washington or at Yale: there was no competition, no clash of egos, no struggle between us. It was as if we were two musicians playing together.

If we found ourselves at a momentary standstill we

would shrug, climb into Steven's car, drive to Berkeley, and eat in the terrace cafeteria at the university. Over lunch in the sun we would start talking again. The ideas would bounce back and forth between us until the problem would be solved. Then we would return to the city to write it down. Even the errands I needed to do with Steven because of my crutches—trips to the doctor, shopping for yellow pads and pencils—were channels for our communication.

When I no longer needed crutches I still needed Steven. A friendship had been formed that gave me steadying emotional and philosophical support. Steven was a therapist for me. As I told him more of my feelings, he began to influence the way I felt about and regarded myself. He pointed out areas of defensiveness and lack of personal faith, including the areas where I felt like an inferior species compared to many others. It was a close emotional relationship that did not include sex, and I felt good that I now was self-accepting enough to form such a friendship.

Steven provided knowledge which came from being born in a different era than I. Steven was perceptive about feelings in ways that I was not. He understood principles of relationships, such as autonomy, in a way far in advance of me. He had a healthy sense of his own pace, the balance of priorities in his life. He regarded sex in a far more natural way than I did. He accepted people's eccentricities without the value judgments that I made, and often with a greater compassion. He could recognize the spiritual in everyday life sometimes more easily than I could, although I had sought this power for a lifetime. I loved to observe him at his house, carefully making tuna-fish sandwiches with green onions and alfalfa sprouts and watching his three cats as they watched him.

Our mutual trust and burgeoning sense of equality allowed me to share power and authority with Steven by inviting him to influence my life. He could be my cosmic taskmaster, telling me when I needed to think more clearly, work harder, go back over a problem. He criticized the doubts I had about my own beliefs, and encouraged me to express my vision with greater faith. He pointed out my evasions and fears of other people and became a prime mover for helping me to overcome these insecurities. He could be a far better connector than I was, when we were on the beach letting the ocean calm us, or on an unfamiliar college campus talking with philosophy students.

To allow a much younger person to function as my parent was a radical innovation—it ignored all the rules of age and status. But I felt a great need for people with authority to influence my life. I needed help to live up to my highest standards, to push ahead against my uncertainties. If we are to find spiritual guidance from other people, we may need to look outside our own family, and to people younger as well as older; we can choose our own "parents," and the ability to choose wisely is essential.

In the afternoons Steven and I would spend a couple of hours at the shore of the Bay or the ocean. We had many places to choose from—the Marina Green, the Golden Gate Promenade, the beach at Crissy Field in the Presidio, Baker Beach, Ocean Beach, the Headlands, Stinson Beach. Having talked all day we would often be silent, watching the gulls or the boats in the channel or the fog blowing in through the Golden Gate or the unexpected flight of a pelican. One day, noticing the bandage which I still required to cover the hole in my foot, Steven looked at me and asked, "Why don't you take off that bandage and try walking in the salt water?" My own belief was that the bandage should always stay on to protect the wound. All my life I had insisted to myself that I was the only one who could be trusted to do things right.

I took off the bandage, and felt the sun and fine sand against my wound, and then the icy chill of the salt water. I walked up and down in the water, the waves splashing against my clothes, feeling a cold clear froth of renewal within me. The water, sand, wind, and sun stirred the cells of my foot to new life.

My friendship with Steven encouraged a deeper healing. I began to experience a relationship without the painful and harmful insecurity that I had always borne. I saw that equality, trust, respect could be taken out of the realm of abstract ideals and made a part of the daily, ordinary exchange with another person. These forms of nurture could serve as powerful, emotionally fulfilling connectors between people whose friendship was based on a shared vision. I realized that the democratic individual was not necessarily separate and mistrustful but a person who had the faith to live respectfully and in a mutually helpful way with others. For most of my life I had been unconsciously and destructively engaged in a war of inequality and insecurity with myself and with other people, even those I loved. Perhaps now my war could cease.

In the summer of 1975 the exhibit of archeological finds from the People's Republic of China came to the De Young Museum in Golden Gate Park. From the first day of the exhibit to the last it was crowded. The visitors were assembled in groups of one hundred outside in the park and then conducted across the roadway and into the exhibit. One Friday afternoon, Steven and I sat for a long time and simply watched the groups go by. They were quiet and serious. There were many types: old people with weathered faces, tourist families, many Asians and inquisitive young people.

We joined the people waiting, and after a while it was our turn to enter the exhibition. It began with human culture of six hundred thousand years ago; the immensity of time awed us. The bowls and vessels were decorated by complex and mysterious designs, by animals, by scenes of early life. There was no pretense, no inauthenticity, no public relations investment in these silent objects; they told their story, they told what people knew and saw and believed. Do we not yearn to be members of a human society that concerns itself primarily with supplying our most elemental needs—food, shelter, human warmth and community, spiritual meaning? People gasped when they came to a reclining figure of a woman, face upward to the heavens; it was a burial suit made out of many pieces of jade, jade believed to ward off evil and preserve the human form, a mysterious and awesome figure of the human submitting itself to a larger destiny. And people came close to tears at the plain pottery figure of a squatting woman, her strong features looking out on the everyday world in which she was born and lived and died.

As I saw in other people the same pain and faith that I felt, and as I shared this with Steven, I increasingly sensed that our individual struggles were parts of a greater movement. I felt that each person's battle for his or her own autonomy is also a battle for all of us, and that we share a political cause far deeper and more fundamental than the clash of political parties and factions. I recognized a continuity in my own lifework from the idealistic boy of the thirties and forties, to the lawyer and reformer, to the person now standing in the park outside the museum.

The major goal of my own work is fundamental, political change. I cannot accept living in a country where people feel powerless to affect their lives. I am unwilling to overlook injustice, cruelty, and oppression. I cannot in good conscience live in a country that imprisons people, humiliates them, degrades them, or ignores their basic humanity. I do not want to live in a country where there is such pervasive cynicism, corruption, and betrayal of its own dignity. I want nothing to do with a country that oppresses the people of any other country. Therefore I want to bring down this system, and replace it with one responsive to human needs. I want to see the economic and social controls returned from giant impersonal institutions to the people. I want a revolution that is embodied in constitutional and legal change—a whole new vision of democratic participation in society. I want to see a sweeping political movement replace those presently in power with people dedicated to new values.

After spending much of my life trying to further political change by legal means, by education, by direct political action, by being part of the new consciousness of the late sixties, I have come to the conclusion that personal growth represents the one and only adequate means of bringing about fundamental political change in this country. Only growth attacks the problem at the source, in our individual conditioning. If we leave our conditioning untouched, every other mode of change, from mild reform to radical revolution, will prove inadequate. These other forms of change may be valid if personal liberation takes place simultaneously. It is frustrating to spend our energy in merely attacking symptoms such as official corruption. The struggle can never be fully effective at this level. Our normal democratic procedure has become ineffective against a system which forecloses real choices. Growth acts directly and needs no permission from the system; when enough people change, the system will be forced to change. Growth is the one political and civic duty that can unite us all. It can be everyone's first task, whatever our other values and priorities. And as growth makes us better connectors, it makes us more sensitive to our needs, to our pain, and to our responsibility to each other, and so we become more directly political in every action that we take.

Because of the nature of the forces we are opposing, the only valid form for a political movement today, I believe, is one that integrates personal growth with the search for political change. In practice, this would mean that those who desire political change also seek their own growth, and work with groups of people who take a continuing responsibility for their own and others nurture. Such a group can provide therapy to those within it, help with the unending battle against conditioning, and provide a nurturing environment without waiting for the remainder of society to change. The group seeks change by offering itself as a model, rather than assaulting other groups and institutions. I think that politics without a nurturing community is alienating in the extreme. But I also believe that personal growth should always have a political dimension. Wholly nonpolitical growth lacks adequate direction. Politically aware growth can seek the autonomy, equality, and community necessary for us to become a more democratic people, whose politics rely not on power over others, but on power over ourselves.

Such a movement would rest upon a radical, revolutionary epistemology which declares that our feelings are factual truth. I formerly believed that my inner world did not supply me with factual knowledge, but was a shadow creation of my mind alone. If I felt pain or insecurity, I failed to consider these as facts that must be confronted. Instead, I thought I could change my feelings by strength of will alone. I did not recognize a real and substantial relationship between my bad feelings and some tangible cause. Therefore my feelings could not be taken in evidence in the court of science or intellectual work or politics or even psychology and education. This lack of belief in my feelings caused a disastrous loss of self-knowledge. The more I was schooled, the less I knew.

The movement toward politically aware personal growth offers a philosophy of liberation by seeking the self-knowledge that society denies us. A revolution of such knowledge cannot be prevented by even the most repressive society. Once this knowledge exists it must spread if it genuinely meets our needs. It would have been so valuable for me to have known more about myself and other people as a lawyer, as an educator, as a member of an institution, in any of the roles and jobs I have had. I see this knowledge as a basic subject in our schools and colleges, for it enlarges our powers as human beings. Many existing sources—some therapies, some new religions and philosophies—offer a segment of it. But the whole body of knowledge is vast and limitless.

Powerful forces, largely untapped by our present society, are available to a movement that integrates growth and politics. Individuals can find a renewed sense of purpose and direction to their lives. There could be the high energy, creativity and fun of working together. Individuals could define their own occupations and professions and still contribute to the overall growth of knowledge and awareness. In contrast to models of rigid tightness among our public officials we could feel permission to become emotionally and physically close to each other whenever possible. I see the movement as a means to bring more love and happiness into my own life.

I believe that as people change, our most basic assumptions about what is possible in society will change too. A society based on different cardinal principles, such as autonomy, sharing, nurture, and community might gradually evolve. If so, it might represent the beginning of a new form of human society, a new social vision achieving ageless humanistic ideals.

The great concerns of today include injustice to oppressed people, the inequality of women and men, the abandonment of democracy and liberty in favor of lawless, authoritarian rule, and the trend toward wanton violence. I believe that change brought about by fighting individual alienation and by growth will directly confront, combat, and overcome these threats to human civilization. All these dangers are perpetuated by the capitalist system with its destructive exploitation of human beings for profit, and its worship of the false idol of exchange value which reduces everything to money and ignores use value or authentic nurture. Marx in his essay "Estranged Labor" pointed to alienation through exchange value and profit as the most fundamental process of capitalism and its chief means of domination. When everything is exchangeable through money, we steadily lose the means of knowing our own needs.

What I propose is nothing less than a revolution

against alienation itself—a revolution that is as necessary in the industrial communist and socialist countries as it is in our own nation. To learn one's own needs and search for sources of nurture is a revolutionary act in defiance of the tyranny of exchange value, the lordship of money. To insist upon equality, openness and nurture in all personal relations is to strike at the heart of exploitation, for as people begin to follow this ideal, exploitation becomes impossible. I believe that democracy can exist free of the capitalist system in a society resting not upon exploitation but upon human needs.

A movement that is also a new way of life offers a meaningful alternative to conventional politics. When we are offered two candidates, neither of whom is acceptable, we do not have to "choose the lesser evil." Instead, we can vote with our entire lives for an alternative society. When the ballot does present one candidate with greater self-awareness, with greater sensitivity to human needs, we can work for her or him. If alienated people are elected to powerful offices, we need not despair. As products of a system that does not rest on true consent, they will find it less and less possible to exercise authority or command respect, and will be increasingly likely to end their terms in office discredited. Other political leaders, more flexible or more aware, will sense the new values and begin to work for them.

I feel it will be possible for a new society to grow up amidst the decay of the old. I can imagine this society beginning as small clusters of people scattered throughout the cities and the country, people who may not even know of other groups similar to themselves. I can imagine these groups gradually discovering one another and sharing what they have learned. No matter what happens to current politics or to established institutions we will eventually have power to end the alien tyranny and replace it with a democratic and humanistic society.

The revolution that the American patriots sought, that the oppressed of the world seek, that Marx sought, that Whitman prophesied, the revolution that offers us a way to survive, proceeds from one human being to the next. Wherever we find ourselves, we are a part of it. Each of us is the leader of her or his own liberation.

How often, seeing how rich and beautiful America is, I have thought, if only it belonged to *all* of us again, if only it was our country. Once again, America could be a haven for its poor and oppressed, and we could be pioneers settling the abused but still fertile land.

Would you like to go to Bolinas with me, on the coast north of San Francisco, and walk along the beach toward Duxbury Reef? From the reef you can look across the Pacific, or back toward the distant city. It is as good a place as I know to find our country and ourselves. Put on a heavy coat—it may be windy and cold.

To reach Bolinas we must cross the Golden Gate Bridge, passing through the arches of its twin towers. The towers are giant Art Deco sculptures, immense futuristic gateways looming up as we drive across the bridge, a reminder of the skyscrapers of New York. For us the towers are portals of time.

Before we cross the bridge, let us pause to read the metal plaque. The inscription gives words to the spirit that the towers express in sculptural form. The bridge was completed in 1937, and to me it is a monument bearing witness to another age—an age of belief, order, faith. Perhaps the deepest human need is to live in an explainable world, a universe where our place can be seen, our purpose understood. The bridge is a testament, not merely to a particular belief, but to the condition of belief, which we seek anew. The inscription dedicates the bridge to the people of California and "to the world at large whose adventurous spirit it reflects":

Lifting its mighty form high above the Golden Gate
It shall testify to the faith and devotion of those who
Undaunted through the years
Sought honestly and fairly through this structure
To tender a definite contribution
To the cultural heritage of mankind

Conceived in the spirit of progress
It shall stand at the gates of San Francisco
A monument to her vision
An inspiration to posterity
And an enduring instrument of civilization
Faithfully serving the needs of a quickening world

As we cross the bridge and pass under the towering arches, we recognize that the spirit of the 1930's was very different from that of the 1970's. The vitality of Art Deco objects and design, science fiction films and literature tell of a people who could imagine the future. In the 1930's there were visions of the future on every hand, from the spire of the Chrysler Building in New York to the Grand Coulee project in the far Northwest to the warnings of films like *Metropolis* and *Things to Come.* Whereas films of today are claustrophobic in their emphasis on crime, cynicism, and separation, films of the thirties made heroes of individuals like Pasteur, Zola, and Dr. Ehrlich. Movies presented the ultramodern men and women of the future: chic, glamorous, amusing, urbane—fantasy people—escapist, yes, but still there was the beyondness. *King Kong* derived much of its power from the contrast between the primitive and the futuristic, showing the immensity of space, distance, and time—so that by seeing far into our beginnings we could also imagine an equally great distance ahead.

A message of the thirties was: problems can be solved, decency triumphs. It was "naïve," but it was also hopeful. There was faith in knowledge, intelligence, and reason. Art Deco incorporated the ancient awe at any advance in knowledge (the discoveries of Mayan astronomers) with modern technology (such as radio communication and rural electrification). Murals portrayed the long march of human history as a story of progress. The skyscrapers were like arrows, pointing upwards.

We pass beyond the bridge, through the rainbow tunnel into the Marin countryside, and onto a small road that rises skyward up the Marin hills along the shoulder of Mount Tamalpais. We come to a crest where we see a panoramic view of the coast and the ocean. Then we descend, first past dark redwoods, then into open country, down to the shore and north until a side road takes us west to Bolinas.

Bolinas is a small village at the beginning of a peninsula that is separated from the mainland by a great lagoon; the beach fronts the ocean on the south. It is a place filled with associations for me, where nature seems moody, wild, and unpredictable, and the people seem close to nature in a respectful and loving way.

If it happens to be a cold, clear, windy day, and the tide

is high, we might do well to have some coffee or even some clam chowder. There is a small unpretentious café where we can sit undisturbed at a table by the wall. We'll need the fortification, and we also need to lose our sense of machine-time, for the place we are going is not really Duxbury Reef but a place in the mind.

We go down to the beach, pausing first to sit on a bench that commands a view of the ocean. It is a traveler's bench, well suited for beginning or ending a long journey.

We start walking west. The tide draws back to let us pass, and the farther we go, the quieter and more subdued we feel, as nature grows larger and civilization drops back behind us. There are cliffs made out of earth and rock to our right, cliffs so organic they look like the beginning of the world. Strange pebbles with holes in them are under our feet; the gulls circle timelessly. We approach a vast silence.

There are omens as we walk. A woman stands facing us and gestures, as if to motion us onward. A man stands near a tree, one that has recently been uprooted from the steep earthen slope, reminding us of nature's awesome power.

It is a primal scene—chaos, the creation—earth sliding down, millions of bugs in the air at one spot, ignoring us. Kelp on the beach, torn loose from the ocean floor, the mud slopes covered with tiny dripping streams, newly fallen rocks all around us, gigantic clouds in the misty distance portending rain. Faces are visible in the pebbles on the beach and the cliffs on the right, timeless, semi-human visages, battered and eroded, with holes for eyes.

We become totally sensual. The brightness of the sun, the smells, the sea spray, the cold, the warmth, the feeling of our bodies as we walk, the soft sand giving way with a squishy sound beneath our feet, the way the wind makes us shiver: all with such intensity that everything we hear, feel or see captures our total attention, pulling us farther along.

We round a corner, and it feels as if we have passed through a gateway into another world. This is an area of natural violence. Sea and earth and weather are in elemental conflict here; this place may look utterly different tomorrow. The towering cliffs may shower rocks down at any time; the sea may reclaim the uncertain strip of sand. We come to a beach that seems to be composed of grey pumice, reminding us of the earth's volcanic origins. Then a brown beach, that looks as if the earliest creatures might have first climbed up from the sea to wriggle across land such as this. Rocks of the reef stretch out on both sides, right and left, making the small lagoon between them tranquil.

With every step the sun grows brighter, the sea more luminous, the clouds more majestic, the earth cliffs more primeval. We are going outwards in time and space. We sit down in the sun and dream, ignoring the showers of tiny pebbles from the cliffs. Time stops, the sea moves but is calm, we no longer feel the wind; our minds drift.

There is a person in all of us that I know about only by knowing that same person inside of me. He is most deeply hidden, but at this place he can appear.

This person has many names. He is the philosopher, the poet, the dreamer. In my own interior world, he is the far-seer. He looks out to sea from Bolinas. He sits in a sunny backyard in the Richmond District of San Francisco, watching the vegetables grow. He stands on the rounded grassy summit of a mountain in the Adirondacks and looks off into the distance. What does he see?

He sees into the future, the beyond. He sees a more

beautiful, sensuous, loving, magical world. He sees a greater vision of human beings, for it is only human beings who can make possible this more dazzling world.

Although I have never believed in any specific religion, I do feel that it is essential to have a vision of human greatness, and one's own greatness. I think this is as essential as food, shelter, or closeness. I think it is a biological need. There must always be a farther place to go. Yet we have become a society which no longer believes in the greatness of men and women, sees civilization as an island in a jungle of human depravity, and tells us all to expect little of ourselves and others, to settle for a small part of what we could be.

Whitman, in the 1855 Preface to *Leaves of Grass,* was braver. The idea of America can never succeed, he wrote, unless the people are poets, unless they show a largeness and generosity of spirit, unless they are lovers of the universe. If Whitman was right and America cannot succeed without greatness in people, then we must be brave enough to show the poet or dreamer or far-seer within ourselves.

Despite all of our denials, I can catch sight of all of us dreaming. I see it in faces at a gay bar, or on the street, or among my friends. I see it in people who are determined to do something creative with their lives, and in people who hold firmly to older faiths. Greatness does not mean success in the system's terms. It means a state of dignity and freedom that everyone has the potential for, an ideal that is deeply American. Listen to Walt Whitman:

". . . This is what you shall do: Love the earth and sun and the animals, despise riches, give alms to every one that asks, stand up for the stupid and crazy, devote your income and labor to others, hate tyrants, argue not concerning God, have patience and indulgence toward the people, take off your hat to nothing known or unknown or to any man or number of men, go freely with powerful uneducated persons and with the young and with the mothers of families, read these leaves in the open air every season of every year of your life, re-examine all you have been told at school or church or in any book, dismiss whatever insults your own soul, and your very flesh shall be a great poem. . . ."

I remember a day on Blueberry Mountain when there were perfect blueberries in limitless quantities, and the day was cool, the sun was bright on the open sloping rocks, and you could just doze off after eating. I remember the taste of the cake with chocolate icing that was served with dinner in the Berkeley Dining Commons, which I would take out onto the terrace and sit with while the sun went down. I remember standing in a great crowd of people in the pouring rain on Broadway and 64th Street in New York to watch FDR drive by in an open car on his last campaign. I remember Paul Robeson's recording of the "Ballad for Americans": "Our country's strong, our country's young, and the greatest songs are still unsung." I remember getting scared listening to "The Shadow" on radio. I remember a great day at my Washington law firm when we got an injunction against post office censorship on behalf of *Playboy* magazine. I remember Leadbelly playing at our elementary school on his twelve-string guitar. I remember giving my speech as editor of our high school newspaper and shaking so that I could hardly read it from the podium of the auditorium. I remember hearing Toscanini conduct in Carnegie Hall. I remember seeing my father happy as he set off rockets on the shore of the lake on the Fourth of July. I remember my mother looking glamorous and beautiful on her way out to theater. I remember what it felt like to be a Supreme Court law clerk, to be a dude on a dude ranch, to be a tense and frightened law student, to be a confident law professor, to be an unnoticed writer in Widener Library at Harvard, to be a famous author who could expect to be recognized in any bookstore in New York, to be the one to lick the peach ice cream off the dasher because I had turned it the longest. I remember how my great-grandmother would point to the long bright streak of reflection from the sun over the water of Long Lake and call it Grandma's Street.

It is so absurd to think that we have used up our world. The whole known universe, reaching beyond our planet to the most distant galaxies that our most powerful telescopes can find, may all be on the inside of one tiny molecule in a conception a billion times larger than our imagination allows. Can there not be equally endless dimensions to knowledge, to feelings, to love?

I now look ahead with fear and hope toward the unfolding of my own life. I do not pretend knowledge of my actual fate. I see that I am capable of having many close relationships with men and women. I can evolve a whole new way of working with people. I can be centered as never before so that I can give the people in my life the utmost freedom. I will keep going in the direction of nature—mentally, physically and spiritually. And I can enjoy the miracle of other people renewing themselves.

Like anyone else, I have felt frightened. My deepest fear is that I will not be able to cope with my life. Sometimes I fear I will never have lasting ties to other people; sometimes I fear ill-health and old age; sometimes I fear the collapse of meaning, so that what I do would have no purpose.

What I have learned is that only by taking risks with

my life can I begin to make it more secure. Nothing outside of myself can promise this security. Only by being stronger, knowing more, being more free, can I find comfort, safety and happiness.

My road travels to places defined not by our alienated minds but by the limitless vision of nature. Along the road I seek knowledge of reality, so that each mile takes me beyond what I have ever known.

I have to grow. I have to be free in ways that people have never been free before. I have to learn what people have never known before. I have to search for the truth as people have never searched before.

I feel an ultimate terror, for I must somehow become greater than I am. Otherwise I will perish here on the rocks. The pressures on me to grow and change are remorseless. How shall I become what I am not, and know not?

And then a calm sweet loving voice says: You have only to learn simplicity. Only to listen. Only to act as you truly feel. Only to believe the thoughts you already have. Only to acknowledge your connection to others, so that their thoughts and energy flow through you, so that their strength and love gives you strength and love to go forward. Only to accept help. Only to give help. Only to move on the current of the universe.

Let us get up from where we are sitting under the cliff and start walking toward the reef. The waves crash on the rocks and send spray that we can feel on our faces; the wind bites, the sun burns.

Now we are standing on the reef itself.

From this hour I ordain myself loos'd of limits and imaginary lines

I put on my magic robe, black and purple with gold and silver stars and moons and zodiac signs.

I inhale great draughts of space

I put on my tall pointed sorcerer's hat.

I am larger, better than I thought

I face the western horizon, the limitless ocean, and bow humbly to all the majesty that is smaller or greater or different than I.

These yearnings why are they?

Then I turn and face the distant city, and the country beyond.

I swear to you there are divine things more beautiful than words can tell

It is open to the farthest horizon.

To know the universe itself as a road, as many roads, as roads for traveling souls

It is a sunny and fertile land where our dreams can come true.

Out of the dark confinement! out from behind the screen!

Here we can be discoverers again, we can explore, we can create a new community, we can experience wonder and magic and love.

Allons! through struggles and wars!

REBEL!

My call is the call of battle, I nourish active rebellion

DOWN WITH THE WALLS
FLEE THE DYING CITY

Allons! the road is before us!

JOIN ME!

Camerado, I give you my hand!

You too shall wear a sorcerer's cloak.

I give you my love more precious than money

That is what human beings can be.

Will you give me yourself? will you come travel with me?

Now it is time to come home from the reef. Walk back along the beach as the day ends. Stop at the place where the road comes down to the beach: there, someone has tramped out in the sand in giant letters, Thank You! Up the hill now, in silence. Calmly and quietly and reverently, let us enter the new world.

The following people took part in the writing of
The Sorcerer of Bolinas Reef:

Michael Guilkey, *Collaborator*
Gregory Marriner, *Collaborator*
James Roediger, *Collaborator*
Roger Ressmeyer, *Collaborator*
James H. Silberman, *editor-in-chief, Random House, Inc.*
Jean Pohoryles, *editor, Random House, Inc.*
Beatrice Bowles, *counselor and friend*
Susan Bruce, *typing and criticism*
Madeline Heinbockel, *typing and criticism*
Alyce Mallek, *typing and criticism*
Susan Scorso, *typing and criticism*
Paul Gamarello, *art director, Random House, Inc.*
Nancy Inglis, *copy editor, Random House, Inc.*
Antonina Krass, *book designer, Random House, Inc.*
Elizabeth Milio, *production, Random House, Inc.*
Carol Atkinson, *typing*
Tim Piland, *typing*
James E. Brogan, *guidance and theory*

Philippe H. Turner, *philosopher*
Christine Delsol, *community interviews and criticism*
Fred Buell, *Whitman 1855 Preface*
Toni Burbank, *criticism*
Melissa Gold, *criticism*
Tom Green, *criticism*
Bob Berlinghof, *criticism*
Peter Munks, *criticism*
Carl Reich, *criticism*
Bob Sedgwick, *criticism*
Sandor Burstein, *medical and spiritual advisor*
Robert Gordon, *medical and spiritual advisor*
S. William Levy, *medical and spiritual advisor*
Allen B. Wheelis, *medical and spiritual advisor*
Sally Guilkey, John Heinbockel, Ken McIntire,
    Sue Munks, *friends, San Francisco*
Jack Post and Greg McIntire, *friends, Marina Nursery*
Kielty and Dayton, Inc., *stationers*
Speedway Copy (Front St., S.F.), *xerox*

A Note on the History of the Book

When I left Washington, D.C., in the summer of 1960, I carried with me the idea for a book that would attempt to understand the course of our society by examining the personal, social and political world that I had lived in for seven years. At Yale in 1960 I began keeping notes. The first draft of "Young Lawyer" was completed in 1965. Then this book was put aside for *The Greening of America,* which I believed had to come first.

In 1970 I returned to this book. The main concepts of personal and societal liberation from alienation date from 1971, and I completed the first draft of "The Turning" in May, 1971. The image of the sorcerer at Duxbury Reef is from Thanksgiving Day, 1971. I wrote the first draft of "Clement Street" in the spring of 1973.

Roger Ressmeyer shared the vision of the book and worked on it for periods of time from the fall of 1973 to the spring of 1976. He influenced its structure and intellectual point of view in important ways, inspired a much higher concept of the late sixties in the third chapter, and held out for higher standards throughout. We began the process of shortening the book to its present length.

In May, 1974, Michael Guilkey joined me, and thereafter we worked together continuously, with Michael serving as a navigator guiding the book toward direct and simple communication with the reader. He was also responsible for adding significantly to the spiritual dimension of the book. James Roediger became a collaborator in May, 1975, and Gregory Marriner in October, 1975. The final version was the responsibility of Michael, James, Greg and myself. The four of us shared in the creative process and became a support group for each other.

All of the experiences in the book are based upon my life, but many events and details have been fictionalized. Some people who appear in the book are wholly fictional, in other cases names have been changed, and in a few instances I have used real names.

Closing lines in italics from Walt Whitman, "Song of the Open Road."

Charles Reich
San Francisco
August, 1976

11/30/76   B112421